Dedicated to the truly decent, compassionate and helpful people who make this world a better place.

All rights reserved
Copyright ©2020 by C L Whitworth
Cover Design Copyright ©2020 by C L Whitworth

Table of Contents

Chef's Notes	3
The Preheat	4
The Left Overs	5
Facts & Stats Succotash	6
Fact Check Fruit Salad	8
"Russia if you're listening"...	10
Collusion Casserole	10
Indictment Omelette	12
GOP Garlic Crisps	14
Shit Storm Sandwich	16
Witch Hunt Elixir	18
Mueller Meatloaf	20
Work Woes Waffles	22
Pinocchio Potato Cakes	24
Reverse Robin Hood Hero	26
Tribal Tripe	28
Roll Back Taquitos	30
Immigration Ice Cream	32
Hail to the Chef Salad	34
AK-47 Apple Pie	36
Russian Roast	38
PsychoGraphics Sushi	40
EPA Muck Stew	42
Pigs-In-A-Blanket	44
Hurricane Ham & Cheese	46
Entitled & Emboldened Chicken Bratwurst	48
Foe Fried Rice	50
Me Too Tacos	52
Democrat Detachment Donut Holes	54
Resignation Rigatoni	56
Sautéed MisInformation Mushrooms	58
Sooper Elite Salad	60
White Privilege Potatoes	62
Trump Base Cheese Burger	64
Comic Mac & Cheese	66
Tumpland Bites	68
Climate Change Chili	70
Polarized Popularity Pizza	72
Literary Lettuce Wrap	74
Melania Melt	76
Free-Press Pepperoli	78
Faith Based Fried Fish	80
Libtard Snowflake Linguine	82
Cult 45 Pale Ale	84
Go Back Baked Alaska	86
K-9 Rump Roast	88
Blissful Beef Burgundy	90
Wait. What? Halibut	92
Mid-Term Mozzarella	94
Tariff Tortilla	96
Rotten Tomatoes	98
Farmer French Toast	100
Stock Market Martini	102
Economical Flatbread	104
Dystopian Daiquiri	106
People Product Pate	108
Global Shift Surprise	110
Berry Bonkers	112
Very Berry Bonkers	114
Meanwhile Mojitos	116
Whistleblower Tea	118
Coup Soup	120
Integrity Iced Tea	122
Testify Teriyaki	124
Law & Order Oatmeal	126
Jaw Dropping Justice Juice	128
Impeachment Pouch	130
Fascist Fricassee	132
FYI Snake Saute	134
Shout-Out Sweet & Sour Peppers	136
Assimilation Artichoke Dip	138
High Tech Biscuits	140
Evolution Edemame	142
Voter Veggie Wrap	144
Lest We Forget Trump Chocolate Cake	146
The Boil Down	148
PARTICIPATE	149

Chef's Notes

About this cookbook: The main purpose of this book is to bring together supposedly opposing parties to gain, insight, understanding. If nothing else, let us come to the table with a sense of commonality and something everybody can relate to and appreciate—food.

I am not a "food person" so to speak. As a matter of fact, I rarely follow recipes and I never even watch cooking shows. I do, however realize the social value and importance of the proverbial "breaking bread" together. Sharing a meal extends a sense of community, acceptance and belonging. It is a strong gesture, not to be underestimated. I invite people from all walks of life, all viewpoints and ideals to sit down and partake, participate and prepare one or two of these delightful dishes. Share a recipe, some food and some ideas. Share viewpoints, compassion and understanding!

About the Recipes: The recipes, for the most part, are to be taken with a grain of salt, so to speak. I do not consider myself to be a connoisseur of any sort, but I am pretty sure all of the recipes are at least somewhat valid, nutritious and safe when used in moderation.

About the Content: The content was captured from the "daily harvest," as I called it. The newsfeeds yielded a plethora of tasty morsels on a regular basis. I will not deny that this project was cathartic. It was a positive way to process the current events. The direction of the country was about to change. I wanted to capture the transition—understand the points of view and hopefully bring people together with insight and understanding.

The headlines, articles and tweets have not been modified. Browse through the real and sometimes shocking news that was obtained through the "daily harvest." Whether you are a Republican, Democrat (or something else) you can find value within theses pages that reflect this historic time in American history and politics.

Disclaimer: I attained most of the content from online newsfeeds (public domain). The content is meant to be used for historical, educational and/or satirical purposes. Contact publishing@persuasivedesign.com for comments. Thoughtful feedback welcome.

The Preheat

"Make America Great Again!" "Build The Wall, Mexico Will Pay" "Cheaper, Much Better Healthcare"
"Bring Coal Back" "Muslim Ban" "End DACA" "End Opioid Crisis" "Best Deals Ever" ~ Donal J Trump

I hope we can look back on this and laugh...

Some people have experienced pure joy and unrestrained glee with the onset of the Trump Administration. White Conservatives who felt they had been "left out" during the Obama Administration were scared and angry, believing immigrants and minorities were receiving welfare and "stealing their jobs." Obama took office during the costly Bush Era Wars and the beginning of the devastating Bush Economic Recession. Times were tough. Many were losing their livelihood, their retirement and their homes in the wake of the Wall Street financial disaster. Obama implemented an Economic Stimulus Plan and imposed new Wall Street Banking Regulations. He offered programs designed to combat the wave of foreclosures, so people could stay in their homes. The economy was badly damaged and it would take years to correct. The ambitious 'Hope and Change' slogan would have to wait until the economy was back on its feet. Once the economy started to repair itself, Obamacare was launched, making affordable healthcare available to everyone including coverage of pre-existing conditions. Obama's Affordable Healthcare Act was deemed to be OK by the Conservatives, but **Obamacare was definitely not**, even though it was the same thing. Obama also increased corporate regulations and Environmental Protection Agency (EPA) standards and regulations. Green Energy Development (tech/production/jobs), was next on the list of 'things to do.'

Towards the end of Obama's two-term presidency, sanctions were put on Russia in response to evidence of meddling in the US 2016 Presidential Election. Malicious misinformation tactics targeted the 'swing states' and the **"Republican Persuadables"** (according to Cambridge Analytica). Although former Secretary of State, Hillary Clinton won the popular vote, the Electoral College awarded Trump, (the inexperienced, new-comer), the Presidency. Most of the nation (world) was shocked as they woke up to the morning news reports of an impending Trump Presidency. This was a presidency that vowed to roll back 'all-things Obama' and they have been doing just that. Pollution standards, fines and enforcement have been reduced while coal/oil production are pushed, instead of green energy. Corporate regulations, and net-neutrality rolled back and Obamacare was to be snuffed out and replaced with (? still waiting). Huge tax breaks for the corporations and the ultra wealthy are considered to be "Winning" for Republicans/Trump Supporters, as his rhetoric and violent suggestions spawned emboldened and violent support.

From that day forward, it seems there has been a non-stop flow of Trump news and incidents ranging from sexual harassment cases to government corruption, immigration 'caravans,' racially motivated hate crimes and mass shootings. The funny thing is...the epitome of the situation lies in the reaction to these events. Democrats are horrified by the lack of oversight, while Republicans feel they are "Winning!" Either way, no one seems to be laughing, nor should they. clw

Trump: Iraq, Syria... whatever. But the chocolate cake was to ...
https://www.youtube.com › watch

Apr 12, 2017 - Uploaded by Repo Man
Trump tells Fox News he told President Xi about the Syrian missile strikes over " the most beautiful piece of ...
▶ 1:00

The Left Overs

Volume 2 of the The Trumpland Cookbook picks up where the first volume left off—with the Mueller Investigation. Volume 2, like the first volume, was written during a tumultuous time. The observations are of the current social climate in the United States, more specifically, the Trump Administration and how it impacts society, public health, corporations, the environment and global politics. By all accounts, this presidency is considered to be very different from previous administrations.

I would like this writing to be considered unbiased and objective—with a dash of 'tongue in cheek'. This cookbook will provide unusual recipes while exposing and examining social behavior patterns and changes. Actual events, as well as opinions and possible solutions to societal problems will be discussed. You may discover a great recipe or even discover a new point of view... If nothing else, I am sure you will at least be outraged, offended, embarrassed, and/or enlightened at one point or another.

USA is deeply divided and battered with "Breaking News" and non-stop 'Twitter feeds.' Scandals, awkward political briefings, protests and even natural disasters are part of everyday news. People are becoming **desensitized** about the amount and seriousness of news events. At this point, it is more surprising NOT to see at least one or two political incidents in the daily news.

Volume 2 picks up at July 2017, 6 months into the Trump Administration. Robert Mueller (appointed by Republican President Bush, retained by President Obama), is tasked to investigate possible 2016 campaign fraud and Russian collusion to influence the US election. "Collusion"—What it actually means and whether it is unlawful, becomes the center-piece 'word on the table.'

The summer of 2017 brought a picinic full of interesting dishes. "The Mooch" (Scaramuccci) Director of Communications was abruptly fired and Paul Manafort was indicted. Trump's personal lawyer and "Fixer," Michael Cohen's house was dramatically invaded and confidential files were ceased. The Stormy Daniel's law suit against Trump commenced, exposing the $130,000 'under the table hush money' paid to her. Trump supporters threatened and injured Trump protesters (some fatally). Later in the year, there were bomb threats (and actual bombs) issued to prominent Democratic Officials and Police Brutality incidents continue. The opioid epidemic takes lives at an alarming rate. Hurricanes ravaged Houston, Puerto Rico and the Bahamas. The West Coast drought fueled massive wild fires that consumed large areas of the California landscape and farmers struggle to operate after the Trump Tariffs.

"Trump-Land" was taking hold and making swift progress. Immigrant Asylum Seeker families are separated and detained indefinitely with grossly inadequate facilities. The EPA staff, prosecutions/fines and environmental protection regulations are greatly reduced. Obama's banking regulations are being rolled back and Obama's Affordable Healthcare Act stalled. Efforts to get the coal industry working again and acquiring public park lands for drilling (fracking) were signs of "Winning" for Republicans. Despite the bad press or "Fake News," there is seemingly nothing Trump can do to make his base lose trust or support for him (so far).

After six months into the Trump Presidency, it was apparent that this administration would continue to be very different from previous administrations in every way. Name-calling and personal attacks are common in Trump's communications—written and verbal. Trump goes 'off-script' to express himself and Trump supporters love it, but a lot of people are horrified to see what they consider to be bad behavior, bad etiquette, lack of professionalism and even "childishness" coming from one of the highest held offices in the world.

Be Informed. Be Aware.

Wash your hands, roll-up your sleeves and dig into this colorful collection of political history mixed with unusual recipes and on-going debates.

Warning: There is A LOT of information in this little 'cookbook.' It may be best to take it one recipe at a time. Skimming over all of it, at one time can be quite daunting.

Side Dish: *The Trumpland Cookbook* (volume 1) was originally published in July 2017, under a different title. The original title was meant to be provocative and demonstrative of societal situations that had extraordinary similarities but for some reason, were considered to be polar opposites. The problem was, the title was too offensive, (especially during escalating racially turbulent times). I opted to change the title to something more generic. Volume 2 was to be published midway through the Trump term but the current title didn't seem to convey the true weight of the current events, so the title was changed once again. The production of *The Trumpland Cookbook* Volume 1 and 2 was a huge endeavor. The shear volume of circulating information was almost paralyzing. As with Volume 1, the nation was bombarded with a never-ending stream of incidents from every direction—everyday. Regardless of the title, *The Trumpland Cookbook,* will remain an important collection of actual headlines, articles and comments from the gamut of news outlets and US citizens who experienced a national and/or personal transition.

1. Make some boundaries for how you consume the news, PLEASE.

Dan Meth / BuzzFeed / Via instagram.com

You can't stay up-to-date on everything. You just can't. You'll

Facts & Stats Succotash

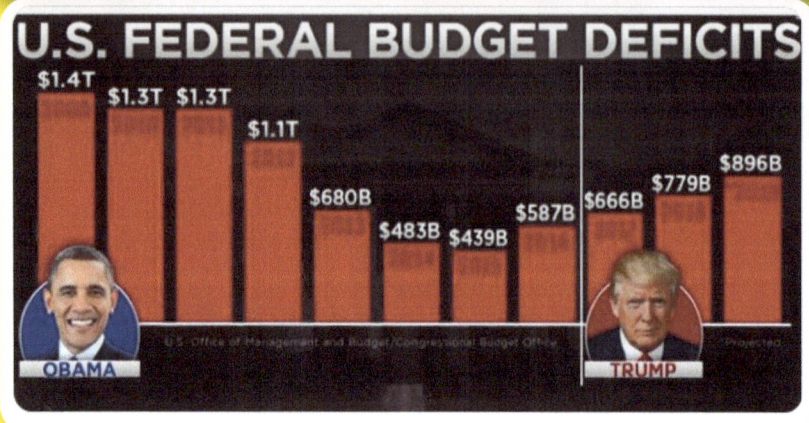

5 Top Promises

- Build a Wall - Mexico Pays
- Repeal & Replace Obamacare
- Immigration Reform Policy
- Military Spending Increase
- "We're All Gonna Be Rich"
- Huge Tax Cuts (easy postcard forms)

Stats & Facts

2016 Presidential Election

- Approximately half (48%) of the nation **did not vote** in the 2016 Presidential Election.
- Donald J. Trump (R) was awarded the presidency by the Electoral College (304 to 227)
- Hillary Clinton (D) received the majority/popular vote (appx. 3,000,000 more votes than Trump)

*stats obtained from US census

	2017	2018	2019
GDP 4Qtr Averages	2.4%	3.0%	2.4%
National Debt	20T	21T	23T
Unemployment Rate	4.8%	4.1%	3.7%
Poverty Rate	12.3%	11.8%	13.4%

Economic Gains (at 3rd year in office): **Clinton 37%, Bush -17%, Obama 55%, Trump 33%**

*stats obtained from MacroTrends

Republican Agenda

"Build the Wall!" (Mexico Pays)
Increase Coal Production and Oil Fracking
Cuts to Medicaid/Medicare
Cuts to Public Education & Social Services
No Equal Rights/Pay for All
No Gun Control
Cut Community Programs
Decrease Environmental Protections
Increase Infrastructure Funding
Increase Military Weapons Spending (a lot)

Democratic Agenda

Invest in High-Tech Border Security
Increase Green Energy (technology & incentives)
Healthcare (affordable or free)
Increase Education (school loan relief/free vocational)
Equal Rights/Pay for All
Gun Control (bkgd checks, no auto assault)
Increase Community Programs Funding
Increase Environmental Protections
Increase Infrastructure Funding
Maintain Military (not increase)

Volume 2 starts July 2017

Facts & Stats Succotash

Ingredients

3 C Canned Corn
1 C Lima Beans or Edamame
1 Tbs Olive Oil
1 Onion, diced
2 Tbs Sherry or Rice Vinegar
1 tsp Sage, ground
1 C Red Bell Pepper, diced

3 Tbs Fresh Basil Leaves, chopped
1 C Baby Spinach, chopped
3 Tbs Hemp Seeds, shelled, raw
1 Tbs Hemp Seed Oil
Pinch of Crushed Red Pepper

Try some Facts & Stats Succotash, it's better than you might think.

Directions

Cook Lima beans according to package directions and set aside. Heat olive oil in a large skillet over medium heat. Add diced onion and peppers, heat until softened. Add corn, vinegar, and Sage. Cook over medium heat another 5 min. Stir in the spinach, basil and cooked Lima beans, heat for a few minutes, remove from heat. Drizzle hemp seed oil and sprinkle hemp seeds, season to taste with crushed red peppers and salt.

Some Current Issues & Main Concerns

Climate change
Tariffs - Broke Farmers
Immigration Policy
Detention Centers (cages)

Opioid Crisis
Foreign Affairs
Russia/Voter Manipulation
Mass Shootings

EPA
Taxes/Rising Deficit
Healthcare
Misinformation

Curious about the validity of a statement, article or news report? You can check it out on FACTCHECK.ORG   Always consider the source(s)

- Republicans primarily rely on FOX News for their information and consider most other news outlets to be "FAKE NEWS." (FOX news is registered as an "entertainment" TV show)

- Democrats tend to listen to several accredited news sources and realize malicious misinformation has been, and will be used to influence potential voters.

Fact Check Fruit Salad

FACTCHECK.ORG

FactCheck.org is celebrating 15 years of holding politicians accountable

Our Mission

We are a nonpartisan, nonprofit "consumer advocate" for voters that aims to reduce the level of deception and confusion in U.S. politics. We monitor the factual accuracy of what is said by major U.S. political players in the form of TV ads, debates, speeches, interviews and news releases. Our goal is to apply the best practices of both journalism and scholarship, and to increase public knowledge and understanding.

- **Warren responded to Facebook on Twitter, telling the company: "You're making my point here. It's up to you whether you take money to promote lies."**

Doubting a Facebook post, something on Twitter, Talk-Show or the News? *Do a little research yourself.*

Always consider the source and check several sources.

MISINFORMATION has become a most unexpected and extremely successful weapon. Nearly every country in the world has been influenced by misleading and/or completely false information. Malicious misinformation has been created and sent out to people who eagerly take-in and then spread false information without checking its validity. There are several 'Fact Check' sources (online) that analyze and rate the validity of statements and articles in the media.

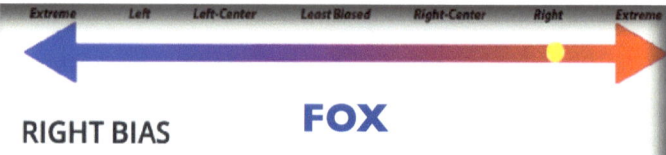

Overall, we rate CNN left biased based on editorial positions that consistently favors the left, while straight news reporting falls left-center through bias by omission. We also rate them Mostly Factual in reporting, rather than High due to misleading information presented by guests as well as a few failed fact checks by TV hosts. However, news reporting on the website tends to be be properly sourced with minimal failed fact checks.

Overall, we rate Fox News strongly Right-Biased due to editorial positions and story selection that favors the right. We also rate them Mixed factually based on poor sourcing and the spreading of conspiracy theories that later must be retracted after being widely shared. Further, Fox News would be rated a Questionable source based on numerous failed fact checks by hosts and pundits, however straight news reporting is generally reliable, therefore we rate them Mixed for factual reporting.

Detailed Report

Detailed Report

Factual Reporting: **MOSTLY FACTUAL**
Country: **USA**

Factual Reporting: **MIXED**
Country: **USA**

Fact Check Fruit Salad

Ingredients

Fruit (washed and cut)
Vanilla Yogurt or
Half & Half Cream

Sweeten with Agave
or Raw Honey

Fact Check Fruit Salad, It's Good For You!

Directions

Wash fruit well in water with a splash of vinegar, rinse again with cold water, drain. Drizzle cream or Almond Milk over fruit - Enjoy the fresh new facts you never knew!

Facebook allows fake ads. Warren took out bogus ad to show up Facebook.

BI Business Insider
Facebook's public push back on Elizabeth Warren's criticism backfires
Facebook tried to make a point about freedom of speech, but Warren shot back and said "It's up to you whether you take money to promote lies."
7 hours ago

DONALD TRUMP
"Hillary Clinton lied many times to the FBI."
— *PolitiFact National* on Tuesday, December 5th, 2017
Trump lied about Hillary Clinton lying - Which she did not.

Trump Doubles Down on Inaccurate Hurricane Forecast

September 5, 2019

President Trump inaccurately stated in his Sept. 1 tweet that Alabama "will most likely be hit" by Hurricane Dorian — a statement that was fact-checked in real time by the National Weather Service. Despite that, Trump has twisted the facts by using an altered forecast map to support his inaccurate tweet.

Williamson Misleads on Children's Health, Vaccines

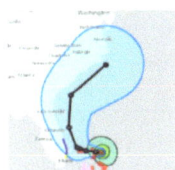

August 20, 2019

In a July 31 television interview, Democratic presidential candidate Marianne Williamson inaccurately implied there might be a connection between vaccines and higher reported rates of childhood chronic diseases. She is correct that reported rates of chronic conditions in kids have increased over the last several decades, but there is no scientific evidence to suggest vaccines are the cause.

Republicans cling to FOX News and rarely (if ever) listen to any other news outlets. They believe only FOX News and what Trump says at rallies even though fact-checking sites have pointed out numerous falsehoods during Trump rallies and interviews.

Democrats are aware of misinformation outlets directed at trump supporters and encourage them to "Watch ANYTHING other than FOX News, just once!"

Collusion Casserole

"Russia if you're listening"...

(During a 2016 Campaign Rally, Trump Asks Russia to Find Hillary Clinton's Emails)

col·lu·sion
/kəˈlo͞oZHən/

noun

secret or illegal cooperation or conspiracy, especially in order to cheat or deceive others.
"the armed forces were working in collusion with drug traffickers"
synonyms: conspiracy, connivance, complicity, intrigue, plotting, secret understanding, collaboration, scheming
"there had been collusion between the security forces and paramilitary groups"

- LAW
illegal cooperation or conspiracy, especially between ostensible opponents in a lawsuit.

"There is no COLLUSION!"

Donald J. Trump @realDonaldTrump

The new joke in town is that Russia leaked the disastrous DNC e-mails, which should never have been written (stupid), because Putin likes me

7:31 AM - 25 Jul 2016

@TeaPainUSA

Trump claims "no collusion" 16 times in a 30 minute interview. Who's he tryin' to convince, us or himself?

12/29/17, 7:23 AM

Collusion Casserole

July 2017

Ingredients

- 6 Potatoes
- 1 Tbs Butter or Olive Oil
- 1-1/2 C Half n Half
- 2 Tbsp Garlic, minced
- 1 Tbs Poultry Seasoning
- 3 Tbs Mayonnaise
- 1/2 C Mushrooms
- 1/2 C White Cheddar Cheese
- 1/4 C Parmesan Cheese
- Fresh Dill

Warm up with a Russian favorite

Directions

Preheat the oven to 400 degrees Fahrenheit. Slice the potatoes, about 1/8 inches thick. Place the potatoes in a baking dish. Melt the butter in a skillet and add the minced onion and the minced garlic. Cook for 5-7 minutes, on medium heat, until softened and slightly golden. Add the cooked vegetables to the potatoes. Season with 1/2 teaspoon salt, ground black pepper, and any combination of dry herbs and/or seasoning mixes that you like. Mix to combine. Heat the half n half until it's almost boiling. Pour over the potatoes. It should barely cover the potatoes. Bake 1- 2 hours at 400°

www.dailykos.com › story › ▾

It's more than a Rumor -- They actually Admitted It - Daily Kos

Aug 24, 2019 - We have all the funding we need out of Russia. ... Foreign money helping make the Trump family what they are today — America's national ...

 Donald J. Trump @realDonaldTrump · 2h
"There is no Collusion. All of these investigations are in search of a crime. Democrats have no evidence to impeach President Trump. Ridiculous!"
@DevinNunes @FoxNews

💬 11K   ↺ 8.7K   ♡ 35K   ✉

MusingsofaMisanthrope @MusingMsAnthrop · 35m
"Russia, if you're listening..."

Tell us again why you specifically asked Russia?

Why not the UK, Costa Rica or any other country.

It seems that the actual definition of the word "COLLUSION" is the problem.

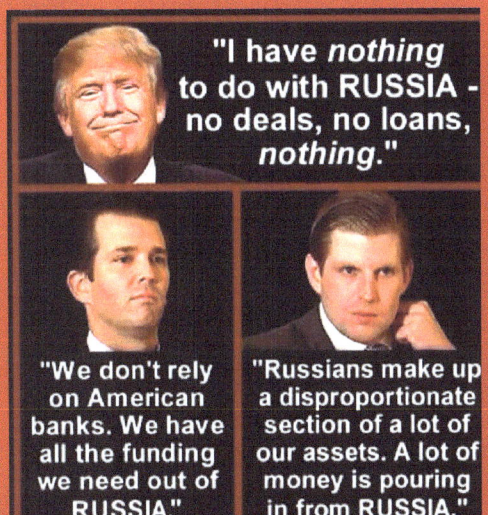

"I have *nothing* to do with RUSSIA - no deals, no loans, nothing."

"We don't rely on American banks. We have all the funding we need out of RUSSIA."

"Russians make up a disproportionate section of a lot of our assets. A lot of money is pouring in from RUSSIA."

Republicans continue to deny any collusion with Russia. NO COLLUSION! NO COLLUSION! NO COLLUSION! NO COLLUSION! NO COLLUSION! NO COLLUSION!...Witch Hunt.

Democrats believe there is evidence of collusion with the Russia government and wealthy Oligarchs. There is also evidence regarding voter manipulation from highly paid 'marketing' companies and foreign entities.

Indictment Omelette

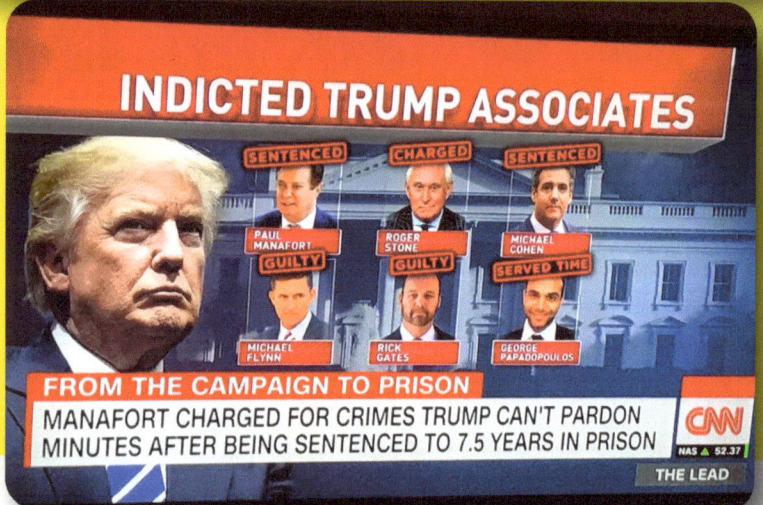

Who has Mueller charged in the Trump-Russia inquiry and who might be next?

David Taylor *and* Sam Morris

Raiding Trump lawyer Michael Cohen is a stunning move by federal prosecutors | @CNNOpinion by @PaulCallan cnn.it/2GNTdnr

Michael Flynn Sentencing Delayed - theminnesotasun.com

Republicans call the Mueller investigation a "Witch Hunt" while Democrats patiently (or maybe not so patiently) wonder who may be indicted next.

politics

More charges could be coming against former Trump aide in Russia probe

Katelyn Polantz, CNN

8:00 PM EST December 5, 2017

FUN FACT

Excerpt from the Mueller Report

encounter with Trump Campaign foreign policy advisor George Papadopoulos. Papadopoulos had suggested to a representative of that foreign government that the Trump Campaign had received indications from the Russian government that it could assist the Campaign through the anonymous release of information damaging to Democratic presidential candidate Hillary Clinton. That information prompted the FBI on July 31, 2016, to open an investigation into whether individuals associated with the Trump Campaign were coordinating with the Russian government in its interference activities.

Indictment Omelette

Ingredients

2 Eggs
1/4C Shredded Cheese
1/4C Green Bell Pepper, diced
1/4C Onion, diced

1 small Tomato (diced)
Fresh Oregano or Cilantro
Crushed Red Pepper
Salt

Directions

Gonna have to crack some eggs for this one. Watch it closely as it heats up, make sure it's thoroughly cooked.

Scramble the eggs and heat in a greased, non-stick pan on medium heat. Spread evenly across pan and sprinkle shredded cheese over egg. Gently add diced veggies to one side of eggs. Fold over and continue heating on low heat until cooked thoroughly. Sprinkle with crushed red pepper and fresh herbs. Salt to taste.

Excerpt from the Mueller Report

On February 16, 2018, a federal grand jury in the District of Columbia returned an indictment charging 13 Russian nationals and three Russian entities—including the Internet Research Agency (IRA) and Concord Management and Consulting LLC (Concord)—with violating U.S. criminal laws in order to interfere with U.S. elections and political processes.[1276] The indictment charges all of the defendants with conspiracy to defraud the United States (Count One), three defendants with conspiracy to commit wire fraud and bank fraud (Count Two), and five defendants with aggravated identity theft (Counts Three through Eight). *Internet Research Agency* Indictment

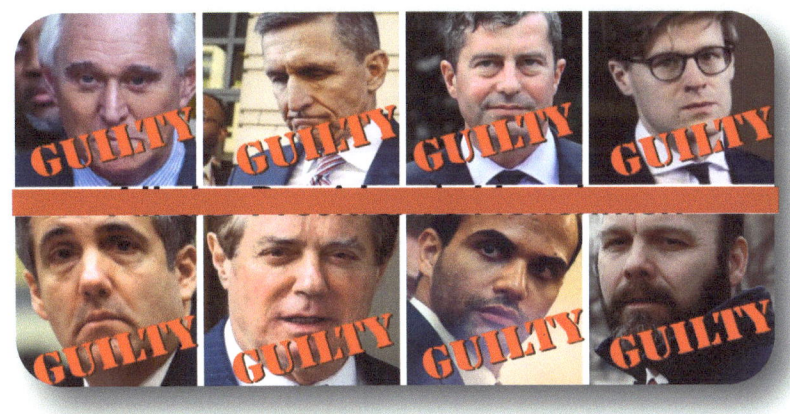

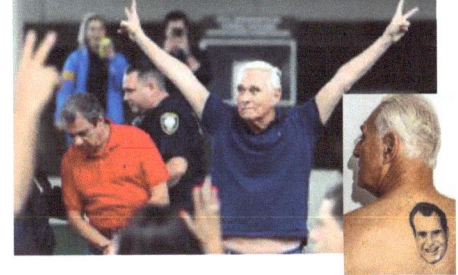

Trump Confidant Roger Stone Indicted

3 days ago
cut business deal in Ukraine ...

Republicans continue to deny any wrong doing and reject all inquiries, investigations or allegations despite the evidence contained in the Mueller Report and the numerous convictions to date.

Democrats want the oversight committee to continue with all investigations and see the Republicans' continued efforts to block investigations as another impeachable offense.

GOP Garlic Crisps

TRUMP IMPEACHMENT INQUIRY · Published 4 hours ago

GOP lawmakers storm closed-door impeachment session, as Schiff walks out

By Ronn Blitzer, Chad Pergram | Fox News

House Republicans seek to enter secure facility for closed-door impeachment interview
Raw video shows Republicans descending towards the facility.

GOP Blocks Obama Gun Control Ploy

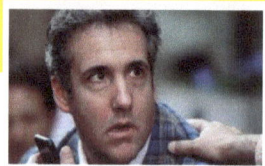

Michael Cohen Was Wiretapped
thedailybeast.com

NPR Politics @nprpolitics

A group of House Republicans broke House rules and disrupted the closed-door proceedings of the impeachment inquiry on Wednesday by entering a secure area without proper authorization.

The GOP

Block Gun Law Vote
Repeal Obamacare
Defund Womens Affordable Health Options (PPH)
Huge Tax Breaks for 1%ers/Corporations
Increase Oil Fracking/Coal Production in USA
Repeal Obama's Wall Street Reform Act
Increase Military Spending
Build Wall (from military funds)
Lessen EPA standards and enforcement
Stop DACA/Block immigrants
Accept $$$ from Russian enterprises (aluminum)
Appoint Numerous Conservative Judges
Block Voter Security

(EVEN IF HE SHOOTS SOMEONE)

BY ANN E. MARIMOW AND JONATHAN O'CONNELL
OCTOBER 24 AT 12:30 AM

NEW YORK — President Trump's private attorney said Wednesday that the president could not be investigated or prosecuted as long as he is in the White House, even for shooting someone in the middle of Fifth Avenue.

Jeff Flake: Fellow Republicans, there's still time to save your souls

Sen. Debbie Stabenow @SenStabenow · 21h
Last week, @SenateDems brought seven bills to the floor that would secure our elections from foreign interference and protect your vote. Senate Republicans blocked all seven!

It is long past time @senatemajldr gets serious about the future of our democracy.

FUN FACT

MusingsofaMisanthr... · 20h
Trump supporters think Flynn is a hero for selling US election info to Russia and Kushner is a hero for selling our Nuclear Tech to Saudi Arabia right now...it says all you need to know about the republicans.

SENATE REPUBLICANS ARE STILL BLOCKING EFFORTS TO SECURE OUR ELECTIONS

 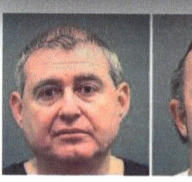 
Giuliani under investigation by fed...

THE TRUMP ADMINISTRATION
THE LATEST NEWS ON PRESIDENT DONALD TRUMP'S PRESIDENCY

White House Orders 2 Former Aides to Defy House Subpoenas

Democrats are challenging the claims of immunity in a lawsuit against former White House counsel Don McGahn
By Mary Clare Jalonick

MusingsofaMisanthr... · 35s
Replying to @jaketapper
It's like 'Gotham' FFS

The GOP is rancid and operates beneath common decency.

Ray Doherty @rayd14... · 11m
Replying to @jaketapper
The whole administration is insane

GOP Garlic Crisps

Ingredients

White Pita Bread
White Coconut Oil
White Garlic Cloves

White Pepper
Seasoning

Directions

*You'll love these simple, light GOP Garlic Crisps
And if you mess it up you can blame it on someone else.*

Slice the GOP pita in half. Spread coconut oil lavishly on every piece. Place chopped garlic on every slice, sprinkle with seasonings. Bake at 375° until crispy (15 min)

The GOP stand strong together, as they 'buck the system' and storm meetings (even though several GOP members were invited and already in attendance). They proudly ignore subpoenas and withhold and/or edit documents and transcripts. More "winning."

FUN FACT

FOX NEWS Report

- Republican GOP continue to back President Trump regardless of alleged wrong-doing. They criticize Democrats for conducting Impeachment investigations and praise Trump for instructing White House Officials to ignore Federal subpoenas and withhold documents.

- Democrats feel there are numerous instances of misconduct and/or crimes committed by Trump and his Administration, including and not limited to; tax evasion, witness tampering, obstruction of justice, extortion, etc.

Shit Storm Sandwich

"I DIDN'T SAY HE WAS A MORON... I SAID HE WAS A FUCKING MORON."

6 days ago
Donald J. Trump's Betrayal of the Kurds ...
thedailybeast.com

US kept no detailed Trump-Putin notes ...
vox.com

Must Reads: John F. Kelly says his tenure as Trump's chief of staff is best measured by what the president did not do

Awkward International Meetings add to the storm...

.@MaddowBlog: Former GOP Rep. Dave Trott says Pres. Trump is "intellectually and psychologically unfit."

"When somebody hurts you, just go after them as viciously and as violently as you can."
Donald Trump
How to Get Rich, 2004

Donald Trump Believed Vladimir Putin over U.S. Intelligence ...
https://www.newsweek.com › World › Donald Trump › International Affairs ▾
Feb 15, 2019 - Donald **Trump Believed** Vladimir **Putin** over U.S. Intelligence, Said North Korea Isn't a Threat Because Russian President Said So: McCabe ...

Harward says no to Trump's national security adviser job, citing 'shit sandwich'

P Politico
Trump claims he's the victim of 'phony emoluments clause'
President Donald Trump on Monday claimed he's receiving unfair scrutiny because of the "phony emoluments clause," as he defended his prior ...
1 week ago

FUN FACT It's a REAL clause

U.S. The Independent
Trump unlawfully declared national emergency to fund border wall, court rules
Donald Trump violated US law when he declared a national emergency over the country's southern border and funnelled taxpayer money...

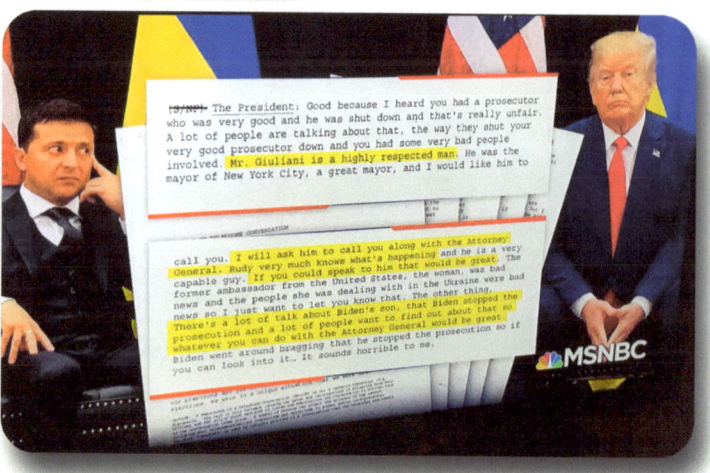

16

Shit Storm Sandwich

Ingredients

2 Slices White Bread

2 Scoops/Slices of... Liverwurst

Try to enjoy this shit-storm sandwich. Its full of it!

Directions

It doesn't really matter how you put it together. It will still amount to a "Shit Sandwich."

The Mercury News
Letter: If I ignored a subpoena, I'd be in handcuffs within hours
Why is it that everyone in the Trump administration is allowed to ignore a subpoena and not go to jail? If I ignored a subpoena, I'd be in ...

NBC NEWS
U.K.'s top diplomat in U.S. blasts Trump in leaked memos
By Linda Givetash and Andrea Mitchell

The memos were critical of Trump's economic policies, claiming they could wreck the world trade system, described conflicts within the White House as "knife fights" and warned "the worst cannot be ruled out" in regard to allegations of Trump's collusion with Russia.

The Hill
Intel Dem: No reason for White House to defy subpoena unless Trump is 'guilty' | TheHill
Asked what would happen if the White House doesn't comply with the subpoena, Heck told CNN, "Defiance of this act constitutes obstruction of

Actor/Painter Jim Carrey Paints a Nightmare Scenario

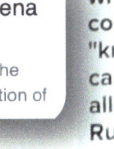
FARMING IN TRUMP COUNTRY
SUPPORT FOR CHINA DEAL?

Business HuffPost
Fed-Up Farmer's Message To Trump: I Wouldn't Vote For You If You Walked On Water
Chris Gibbs, a former Republican county chair in Ohio, says he's done with Donald Trump.

Trump claims a victory in China trade war, but US farmers want details
AFP

Farmers Turn Backs On Trump
HuffPost

- Republicans muddle through the storm of high turn-over and record resignations within the Trump Admin. They are left with being sorely understaffed and unqualified to deal with national/internation business, emergences and political scandals.

- Democrats are thinking the GOP plan is to create so much corruption it is simply too much to notice and/or deal with.

Witch Hunt Elixir

Donald J. Trump ✓
@realDonaldTrump

WITCH HUNT!

6:51 PM · Jan 26, 2019 · Twitter for iPhone

Thorsten @Airvooocht · Jan 27
Replying to @realDonaldTrump
This 'WITCH HUNT' has...

- 199 criminal counts
- 37 indictments
- 7 Guilty pleas
- 4 prison sentences
- 1 Cohen convicted of 8 felonies
- 1 Manafort convicted of 9 felonies
- 1 Roger Stone arrested

Republicans say the Mueller investigation is a "Witch Hunt" and is wasting tax-payer money. They accuse Democrats of simply being vindictive and say "collusion" isn't a crime anyway.

• • • • • • • • •

Democrats see reasonable cause to investigate possible Trump-Russian ties that may have led to unjust emollients enrichment, election meddling and obstruction of justice.

THE ILLUSIVE "INDIVIDUAL #1"
Donald J Trump

Michael Cohen, the president's longtime lawyer who testified before the House oversight committee last week, is asked to produce "any audio or video recordings of any conversation with or relating to the Trump Campaign, Donald Trump or his Business Interests from June 2015 to the present. See below for the full list of people and groups that received document requests from the committee:

Persons of Interest (as noted in the Mueller Report)

Alan Garten	George Nader	
Alexander Nix	George Papadopoulos	Ronald Lieberman
Allen Weisselberg	Hope Hicks	Sam Nunberg SC
American Media Inc	Irakly Kaveladze	Group Limited
Anatoli Samochornov	Jared Kushner	Sean Spicer
Andrew Intrater	Jason Maloni	Sheri Dillon
Annie Donaldson	Jay Sekulow	Stefan Passantino
Brad Parscale	Jeff Sessions	Steve Bannon
Brittany Kaiser	Jerome Corsi	Ted Malloch
Cambridge Analytica	John Szobocsan	The White House
Carter Page	Julian Assange	Trump Campaign
Columbus Nova	Julian David Wheatland	Trump Foundation
Concord Management and Consulting	Keith Davidson	Trump Organization
	KT McFarland	Trump Transition
Corey Lewandowski	Mark Corallo	Viktor Vekselberg
David Pecker	Matt Tait	Wikileaks
Department of Justice	Matthew Calamari	58th Presidential
Don McGahn	Michael Caputo	Inaugural Committee
Donald J Trump Revocable Trust	Michael Cohen	Christopher Bancroft Burnham
Donald Trump Jr.	Michael Flynn	Frontier Services Group
Dylan Howard	Michael Flynn Jr.	
Eric Trump	Paul Erickson	J.D. Gordon
Erik Prince	Paul Manafort	Kushner Companies
Federal Bureau of Investigation	Peter Smith (Estate)	NRA
	Randy Credico	Rick Gates
Felix Sater	Reince Priebus	Tom Barrack
Flynn Intel Group	Rhona Graff	Tom Bossert
General Services Administration	Rinat Akhmetshin	Tony Fabrizio
	Rob Goldstone	
	Roger Stone	

TRUMP DEFIES CONGRESS
- Tells W.H. official: don't comply with subpoena
- Files lawsuit over House demand for financial records
- Declines House request for tax returns
- Plans to fight House subpoena for McGahn
- Says Stephen Miller will not testify on immigration

MusingsofaMisanthrope @MusingMsAnthrop · Dec 1
Replying to @politico
If only trump had messed around with an intern...

instead of rigging an election, committing national security breeches, compromising American assets, initiating malicious misinformation...oh, and all that bribery, extortion and money laundering...

It would be so much easier.

Witch Hunt Elixir

Ingredients

1 liter Dr. Pepper
Spiced Rum
Vanilla Vodka
Ice from a Glacier

Herbal Drops
St. John's Wort
California Poppies
Licorice Root

Calm yourself and foresee the future with this intoxicating elixir

Directions

Swirl it all together and pour it over ice.
Add a sprig of fresh mint and Eye of Newt for the full effect.

Which is the Witch Hunt?

The President fired Comey abruptly without offering him an opportunity to resign, banned him from the FBI building, and criticized him publicly, calling him a "showboat" and claiming that the FBI was "in turmoil" under his leadership. And the President followed the termination with public statements that were highly critical of the investigation; for example, three days after firing Comey, the President referred to the investigation as a "witch hunt" and asked, "when does it end?" Those actions had the potential to affect a successor director's conduct of the investigation.
~Excerpt from the Mueller Report

INVESTIGATION SCOREBOARD:

 Whitewater "Investigation" 6 years — 0 indictments — 0 convictions

 Benghazi "Investigation" 4 years — 0 indictments — 0 convictions

 Hillary Email "Investigation" 2 years — 0 indictments — 0 convictions

 Trump-Russia Investigation 1 year — 19 indictments — 5 guilty pleas — 4 convictions

ENOUGH SAID.

FUN FACT

FBI clears Clinton -- again - CNNPolitics

HILLARY CARD

DEFLECT BAD NEWS AWAY FROM TRUMP. SWITCH TO HILLARY.

USE HILLARY CARD WHEN YOU LACK ANY ACTUAL ARGUMENT.

- Republicans seem to believe that the Russian investigation is a "WITCH HUNT" fabricated by the "Deep State," an inside-government scheme run by the FBI/CIA. They continue to demand more HRC investigations and still chant "Lock Her Up!" at Trump rallies.
- Democrats don't see the logic of the "Witch Hunt" accusations because several members from the Trump Admin have already been found guilty and it was the FBI who investigated HRC and sprung the damaging HRC email announcement just before the 2016 election. (spooking tentative HRC voters).

Mueller Meatloaf

The Mueller report is 448 pages.
chicagotribune.com

Robert Mueller - US Department of Justice, Special Counsel, Director of the FBI, 2001-2019 War Veteran, Republican - conducted the 2-Year Russian Investigation

Mueller appointed by Bush, retained by Obama. He has an impeccable reputation throughout his career. FBI officials are deemed impartial and swear an oath to uphold justice. Both Republicans and Democrats hold Mueller in high regard because of his high level of integrity and thorough investigations.

Trump Said Probing His Finances Would Be A 'Red Line.' That's Exactly What Robert Mueller Is Now Doing.

Mueller has asked Deutsche

DONALD TRUMP STILL FACES DOZENS OF ONGOING INVESTIGATIONS AFTER MUELLER PROBE: 'HE BY NO MEANS IS SAFE'
BY ALEXANDRA HUTZLER ON 7/25/19 AT 2:07 PM EDT

FUN FACT
It doesn't work that way.

Trump Jr. cites attorney-client privilege in not answering panel's questions about discussions with his father

By Kyle Cheney | Dec 6, 2017

MONDAY APRIL 9 42°

TOP STORIES

Trump lawyers want second special counsel appointed now

Mike Allen DEC 12, 2017

Republicans accused of concocting email scandal against Robert Mueller

Trump slams FBI for raid of his personal attorney's office

Mueller Meatloaf

Ingredients

- 1 lb Hamburger
- 1 Egg
- Bread Crumbs
- Hickory BBQ Sauce
- Worcestershire Sauce
- Onion soup mix (dry)

Enjoy this meaty report...I mean dish. It may take some time to process...

Directions

Mix the hamburger and egg well. Add breadcrumbs and dry soup mix. Mix well and press into baking pan or dish. Top with BBQ sauce and bake at 325° for approximately 40 mins. Broil for 5 minutes to sear if desired.

Much of the Mueller Report was "redacted" (blacked out), to protect on-going criminal investigations. Mueller was told by the DOJ (Barr) that a sitting President can not be indicted. When he was asked if Trump could be indicted after his time in office, Mueller's prompt response was "True."

Mueller Report: Conclusions - ...

impeachment remain after Mueller ...
abcnews.go.com

Republicans 'cry foul' as the Mueller Investigation gets underway. They consider the investigation to be a "Witch Hunt" and a waste of tax-payer money. They also say it will inhibit the President from doing his job.

Democrats feel it is their responsibility to investigate the possibility of election hacking, obstruction of justice and government corruption. They believe the oversight committee should fulfill their civic duty.

Work Woes Waffles

British MP 'stunned' at anti-Muslim Trump tweets
2:46 PM EST November 29, 2017
Video 03:32

politics

Trump's behavior raises questions of competency

Analysis by Stephen Collinson, CNN

Updated 2:25 PM EST November 29, 2017

NBC NEWS
A Panama tower carries Trump's name and ties to organized crime

TOP STORIES

CNN — **FUN FACT**
North Korea: New missile test shows all of US in range

NOVEMBER 12 58°

TOP STORIES

The Washington Post
Former U.S. intelligence officials say Trump is being 'played' by Putin

NBC NEWS
President Trump seems to slur words in speech, stirring speculation

CNN
Kushner testified he did not recall any campaign WikiLeaks contact

engadget
Pentagon left public intelligence gathering data on exposed server

FUN FACT
Did President Trump admit to obstructing justice in new tweet? | Sun, Dec 03

CNN
Trump says he believes Putin's election meddling denials

Work Woes Waffles

Ingredients

- 2 Eggs
- 1 1/2 C Flour
- 1 Tbsp Sugar
- 4 tsp Baking Powder
- 1 3/4 C Milk
- 1/4 cup Vegetable Oil or Coconut Oil

Work can be so woeful sometimes... Feel better with Work Woes Waffles.

Directions

Heat waffle iron. In large bowl, beat eggs with wire whisk until fluffy. Beat in remaining ingredients except berries just until smooth. Pour slightly less than 3/4 cup batter onto center of hot waffle iron. Close lid of waffle iron. Bake about 2 minutes or until steaming stops. Carefully remove waffle. Serve immediately. Top with fresh berries. Repeat with remaining batter.

FUN FACT More than half of the original White House staff has been fired or resigned, leaving under-qualified personnel who are loyal to Trump under all circumstances.

politics
The 13 most bizarre lines in Donald Trump's Thanksgiving speech

CNN
There's a massive moral vacuum in the country right now

Newsweek
'Are You Stupid?' Donald Trump's Tweets Just Gave These Lawyers Ammunition for Their Court Case Against His Administration

The Washington Post
BIG MACS, SCREAMING FITS AND CONSTANT RIVALRIES
Scenes from the Trump campaign

Republicans are still proud of their leader. They offer him loyal support and adoration despite numerous misspeaks, lies, scandals and investigations. Trump's approval rating has gone as low as 35% nationwide but remains in the 90s for Republican voters.

Democrats are amazed at what they see as being a very low level of knowledge, ethics and behavior from both the Trump Administration and his base.

Pinocchio Potato Cakes

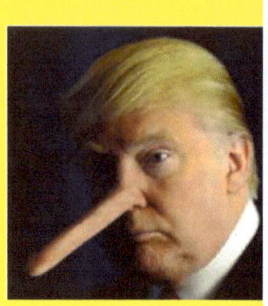

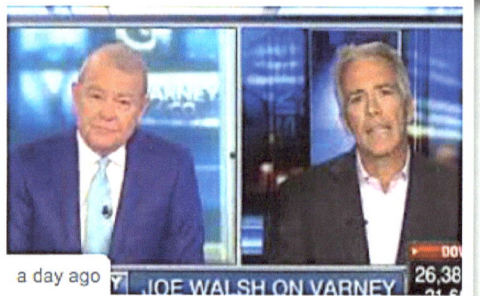

Walsh: Do you believe Trump has ever lied to his base?
Varney: No, never.

Misinformation

"Alternative Facts," Untruths and Lies from trusted officials or public news source is a toxic malignancy that increases divides and erodes society at the core. A society without integrity will inevitably collapse in on itself as corruption increases.

clw

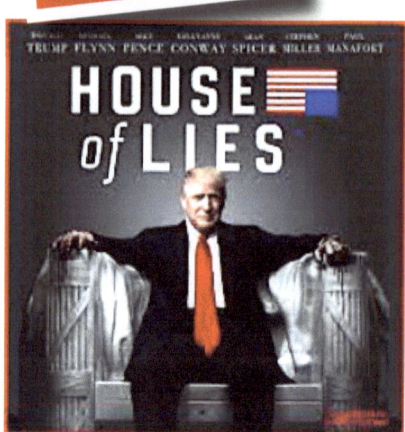

Trump officials keep contradicting each other trying to explain why they are separating children from their parents at the border

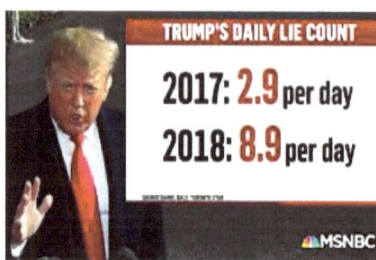
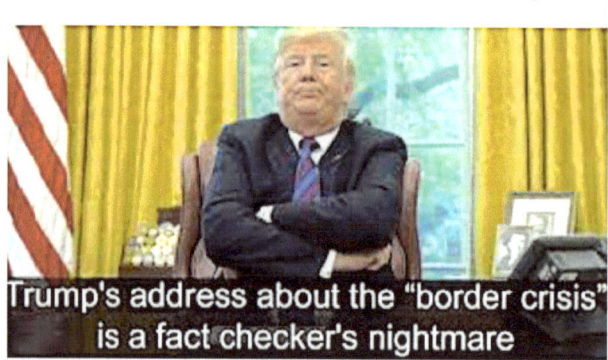

Pinocchio Potato Cakes

Ingredients

1 Egg
3 Tbsp Flour
6 Potatoes, shredded
1/4 Shredded Parmesan Cheese
1/2 C Onion
1/4 Vegetable or Coconut Oil
1/2 tsp Garlic Powder
1 tsp Chives, chopped

Just sit back and enjoy some Pinocchio Potato Cakes and be sure to keep count.

Directions

In a large bowl, beat together eggs, flour, baking powder, salt, and pepper. Mix in potatoes and onion. Heat oil in a large skillet over medium heat. Working in batches, drop heaping tablespoonfuls of the potato mixture into the skillet. Press to flatten. Cook for about 3 minutes on each side until browned and crispy.

FUN FACT

Trump Lies Don't Bother Some People ...
lamag.com

Sarah Sanders Says Trump Never Advocated Violence.

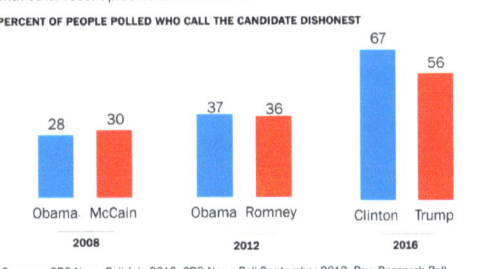

President Trump shows doctored hurricane chart. Was it to cover up f...
President Trump had erroneously stated Hurricane Dorian threatened Alabama last week.
washingtonpost.com

Republicans probably don't know when they are getting 'Fake News' because they tend to be loyal to one news source - FOX... or "FAUX News" as liberals affectionately call it.

Democrats tend to listen to a variety of news sources, and are aware of the running tally of Trump Administration misspeaks...

Reverse Robin Hood Hero

A Hasty, Hand-Scribbled Tax Bill Sets Off an Outcry

By JIM TANKERSLEY and ALAN RAPPEPORT
DEC. 1, 2017

With Republicans intent on passing a tax overhaul along party lines, public protests have been Democrats' only weapon throughout the lightning-fast progression of the bill.

POLITICO

Congressman Tim Ryan @RepTimRyan

This can't be swept under the rug: Trump is making cuts to SNAP—taking food away from 3.1 million Americans, including 500,000 children. And this harmful rule will affect over 100,000 Ohioans. They need to reverse this decision immediately. #HandsOffSNAP

> Flint doesn't have water.
> Puerto Rico doesn't have power.
> We "can't afford" Meals on Wheels.
> But sure. Let's give millionaires & billionaires the largest tax cut in United States history. I'm sure they'll put it to good use.

"You all just got a lot richer," President Trump told friends dining at Mar-a-Lago Friday night, hours after signing tax overhaul into law

Tweet your reply

Corporations and people making over $500,000/yr are happy to get a record tax break of up to 35%

Policy: Money
'Holy crap': Experts find tax plan riddled with glitches

Some of the provisions could be easily gamed, tax lawyers say.

By Brian Faler | Dec 6, 2017

CNN
Republicans release their final tax bill ahead of key vote

Vox

We're witnessing the wholesale looting of America

Unchecked by norms or political prudence, it's smash-and-grab time for the GOP.

By Matthew Yglesias | December 19, 2017 8:40 am

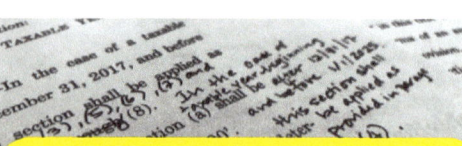

> The tax bill provided an opportunity for President Trump to show his priorities. But so much of it is traditionally Republican and doesn't offer the kind of help for the working class he promised.

Bernie Sanders @SenSanders

It is a disgrace that Republicans are rushing to pass a massive tax break for the wealthy while children are about to be thrown off their health insurance.

The Washington Post
Senate passes Republican tax plan in major win for Trump and party leaders

Reverse Robin Hood Hero

Ingredients

- Bologna, Salami, Ham
- Mayonnaise
- Italian Salad Dressing
- Shredded Lettuce
- French Bread Bun
- Tomato sliced
- American Cheese
- Red Onion
- Italian Seasoning
- Salt & Pepper

While the rich get richer, you can enjoy top shelf ingredients for your Reverse Robin Hood Hero

Directions

There has not been one public hearing, no opportunity to hear from economists, governors, mayors or ordinary Americans who will be impacted by this tax bill. This is a sham.

Mix together the mayonnaise and Italian salad dressing. Brush cut sides of bread with dressing mixture. Fill bread with lettuce mixture, meat, tomatoes and American cheese. Sprinkle with seasons to taste.

Dems Erupt In Anger After 'Corrupt' Tax Bill Passes The Senate

"This corruption is hollowing out America's middle class & tearing down our democracy," Sen. Elizabeth Warren tweeted.

Bernie Sanders @Sen... · 2h
Ted Cruz and Tim Scott should listen to these Patriotic Millionaires instead of their campaign contributors.
#TaxDebate

BBC News (World) @B... · 1d
US homeless people numbers rise for first time in seven years

CNN
Warner: Voting on GOP tax reform 'my single worst day as a US senator'

FUN FACT

Republicans rushed to push through a tax bill in the middle of the night with hand written scribbles with inadequate wording but it accomplished their main goal of providing huge tax breaks to the wealthy.

Democrats were out-raged at the undercover and rushed process. They were given over 500 pages to review over-night before having to vote on the tax bill. Republicans controlled the house and senate so the bill passed with the needed number of votes despite total Democratic opposition.

Tribal Tripe

Primitive Tribal Mentality (PTM)

trib·al·ism
/ˈtrībəˌlizəm/

noun

the state or fact of being organized in a tribe or tribes.

- DEROGATORY
  the behavior and attitudes that stem from strong loyalty to one's own tribe or social group.
  "a society motivated by cultural tribalism"

Some people are prone to 'Tribal Mentality' behavior. They gain a sense of primal security by associating only with people who resemble themselves. They tend to be 'on-gaurd' and fearful of other groups [getting *their* resources]. They foster a 'group mentality' where they believe and support their 'leader' without question. They isolate themselves against open-mindedness and information that threatens their point of view. The more they believe their resources are threatened, the more they become possessive and lash-out. "I don't care what you say, it's US against THEM!"

The opposite of Tribalism may be considered Socialism, in the sense of fostering a diverse and cooperative community that share resources. People interact with each other on an individual basis as opposed to some sort of group affiliation or physical appearance.

People with over-active Amygdalas (the fight or flight mechanism) tend to perceive more things as being a threat to their security, than people with less active Amygdalas. The Amygdala has been called the "lizard brain." This term refers to the primitive nature and necessity of the Amygdala to allow you to identify and react to possible threats. Tribes had to stick together for protection and survival. Quick identification of 'friend or foe' was paramount. It is a primitive 'knee-jerk' reaction.

As societies grew larger and more interactive, it became apparent that the sharing of knowledge and resources was beneficial to all. The human race evolved into more of an extended community as opposed to segmented and isolated groups. Ironically the defensive and/or destructive 'Tribal Mentality' behavior isn't the default behavior exhibited by most toddlers. The fight or flight mechanism still resides in us all, but is more active or more easily triggered, in some, as opposed to others. Tribal behavior is more so, taught at an early age, reinforced and perpetuated. People with less active Amygdalas don't feel as threatened by other types of people and have the ability to think independently—sometimes even questioning the behavior and ideals of their own 'tribe'' - Intellectual Evolution.

CLW

Tribal Tripe

Ingredients

Tripe
Butter
White Flour
White Milk
White Onion, diced
Salt and White Pepper

Put your torches down and take time to enjoy this pale, white tripe, just the way you like it.

Directions

Boil the tripe squares in water for 15 minutes then drain. Add the onions and enough milk to cover and cook for two hours over low heat. Melt the butter and flour together and stir to create a thick paste then slowly whisk in the milk form the tripe to create a white sauce. Season well with salt and pepper. Add the tripe squares, reheat and serve. Use whatever amounts you want. DON'T TREAD ON ME!

darpo
@MizterMordant

Replying to @bubbagump324 and @Jen_C_

You look at these people and instinctively know they are incapable of intelligently, or even rationally, discussing Trump. Not only do they lack knowledge of the facts and issues, but they have the conversational skills of a queef.

8/2/18, 4:40 PM

kodibear
@alkikodibear

Replying to @washingtonpost

Who didn't know that before November 2016? His base certainly knew. Back then they had I love Russia buttons after Trump asked Russia to hack Clinton. Currently they show up at rally's wearing tee's reading they'd rather be Russian... (vox ohio rally)

Trump Supporters Love Chaos as Much as ...

Republican demographics show many are religious. Some are homophobic, xenophobic and/or racist. They feel an overwhelming need to protect themselves by stock-piling guns and ammunition. They feel threatened and band together in look-alike groups with an 'us against them' mentality.

Democrats operate in socially diverse groups. They usually don't feel threatened and they don't feel an over-whelming need to stockpile weapons or discriminate against others.

Roll Back Taquitos

Rolled Back Items:
- EPA Standards and enforcement
- Wall Street Banking Regulations
- FEMA budget & Staffing
- Community Service Programs
- Education Funding
- Opioid Crisis Funding
- Internet oversight/regulations
- Planned Parenthood Healthcare
- Womens Reproduction Rights
- College Debit Relief
- CDC/HIV staff

E.P.A. Blocks Obama-Era Clean Water ...
nytimes.com

The Washington Post
The FCC is expected to repeal its net neutrality rules today, in a sweeping act of deregulation

BBC NEWS

Debt relief for defrauded students halted under Trump, says report

⏱ 12 December 2017   US & Canada

83

83 Environmental Rules Being Rolled Back Under Trump - T
https://www.nytimes.com › climate › trump-environment-rollbacks
Jun 7, 2019 - All told, the Trump administration's environmental rollbacks could .....

Trump Signs Biggest Rollback of Bank Rules Since Dodd-Frank ...
https://www.bloomberg.com › news › articles › trump-signs-biggest-rollba... ▾
May 24, 2018 - President Donald Trump has signed the biggest rollback of financial regulation

🅽 NBC NEWS
Trump breaks out the gold scissors to tout deregulation

Republicans are On-Track for Rolling Back as Much of Obama Era Bills and Legislation as Possible.

Less Oversight, Less Banking Regulation and Less Pollution Regulations.

Trump rollback of banking regulation ...
nst.com.my

Roll Back Taquitos

Ingredients

Meat of your choice
1/2 tsp Garlic Salt
1/2 tsp Cayenne Pepper
1 tsp Cumin
Corn or Flour Tortillas

Guacamole
Pico de Gallo or Salsa

Sour Cream,
Cilantro, chopped

After rolling back so much, you want to roll-up some Roll Back Taquitos.

Directions

Cook meat on skillet, mix in the seasonings. Put the meat on the tortilla, tuck in the edges and roll in to tight rolls. Bake at 400° on flat cookie sheet for 10-15 minutes. Remove and serve with Pico de Gallo, sour cream, Cilantro, guacamole and tomato.

Trump Rolls Back Obama's DACA Program

If you were born here, you can stay here. This is your home.

Not Anymore under Trump

Julie Brethauer
@JulieBrethauer

Replying to @IndivisibleNap @SassyCanadianCk and @MarkTully20

I was absolutely mystified at the MAGA's replies to the announcement that he rolled back vehicle emissions level requirements in California. They were actually cheering the fact that it's ok to put more pollution in the air.

And they call US deranged?!? Unbelievable 😡

The Root

Trump Administration Diverts FEMA Disaster Relief Money to Keep More Migrants in Cages

Trump Administration Diverts FEMA Disaster Relief Money to Keep More ... the federal government hostage over funding for his border wall.

The Internet is becoming less free, less trustworthy, and more subject to government manipulation around the globe.

NPR @NPR

The United Nations is investigating extreme poverty in the U.S. One sign of it in Alabama? The re-emergence of hookworm.

Republicans are winning as they roll back environmental protection, banking/corporate regulations and over-sight. They are especially happy to have community program funding cut, gun laws loosened, women's rights and DACA rolled back.

Democrats are horrified to hear that EPA standards/regulations are being cut back, along with women's rights and wall street banking regulations lifted. More 'Robo calls' and internet fraud are not great either....
(net neutrality reversed)

Immigration Ice Cream

Where are they??

The US Has "Disappeared" More Than 42,000 Migrants. Where's the ...
Trump's most insidious immigration program is operating under the radar.
🔗 truthout.org

Separated families, held indefinitely in cages without proper food, medication, hygiene supplies or bedding.

"Somebody Is Going to Die": Lawyer ...
democracynow.org

"Senate GOP plans to divert health, education funds to border wall"

Senate GOP plans to divert health, education funds to border wall
rollcall.com

11:29 AM · 8/12/19 · Twitter Web App

IMMIGRATION
THE TRUMP ADMINISTRATION MIGHT END REFUGEE RE-SETTLEMENT AS WE KNOW IT

Stephen Miller is leading the White House's potential plan to decimate refugee admissions to the U.S.

BY ALISON DURKEE
SEPTEMBER 6, 2019

6 days ago
photo of an 'immigrant child ...
wgntv.com

ICE arrests nearly 150 workers in raid ...
news5cleveland.com

up tp $775 Per Detainee - Per Day
Over 30,000 Detainees = $$$ PER DAY
WHERE is the $$$ Coming From?
WHO is Getting the $$$?
HOW is the $$$ Being Used?

ICE Raid in Mississippi Food Plants ...

msnNOW
'Don't open the door': US activists organize to thwart ICE
Though she speaks little English, Yoana was calm when two officers from the US federal agency tasked with deporting undocumented people ...
2 days ago

Immigration Raid ...
wvpublic.org

32

Immigration Ice Cream

Ingredients

- 1 Tub Mint Chocolate Chip
- 1/4 Cup Milk
- Walnuts
- Chocolate Rice Crispies
- Dark Chocolate Syrup

Directions

So sweet, so simple so comforting to some but a dream to others. Enjoy it while you can.

Get a nice big dish, scoop out desired amount of ice cream. Pour milk over and cut in with spoon. Sprinkle rice crispies and pour chocolate syrup over all over, like none of this matters.

ICE agent dumps out water left for families crossing the desert

June 20, 2018, 2:30 AM MDT / Updated June 20, 2018, 5:45 AM MDT
By Julia Ainsley

WASHINGTON – The cost of holding migrant children who have been separated from their parents in newly created "tent cities" is $775 per person per night, according to an official at the Department of Health and Human Services – far higher than the cost of keeping children with their parents in detention centers or holding them in more permanent buildings.

This is Melanija Knavs
- Dropped out of college
- Came to the U.S in 1996 on an B1-B2 visitor visa. Per AP, illegally took 20k for "modeling work"...
- Allegedly worked as a high paid escort
- Married crusty old man 23 years her senior for money
- Lied about having a degree from the University of Slovenia
- Allegedly speaks 5 languages but there is no video evidence of her speaking anything but broken English

Republicans blame the asylum seekers for attempting to seek shelter legally and/or illegally. Their main concern is to keep immigrants out. "Build the Wall!"

Democrats realize the extreme conditions someone would have to go through to leave hour home behind and travel across a desert. They believe in immigration policy, with high tech border security, due process and humane treatment of detainees.

Hail to the Chef Salad

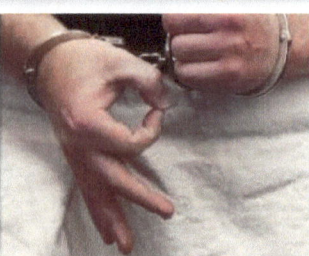

White Nationalism & Resisters

White Nationalists ban together in tribal groups while 'Resisters' express their disdain with an individualistic flip of the finger to the Trump Administration and Trump Supporters.

Many Trump Supporters are motivated by tribal instincts and encouraged by the Trump Administration. They see diversity as a threat to themselves and their resources. They act hostile and defensive towards anyone who doesn't look like them or believe what they do. It should be noted, however, that even if their world was all white, their tribal mentality would then focus on different tribal delineations such as different religions, sports fans, or origin (Catholics vs Protestant, Raiders vs Cowboys, England vs Ireland).

They swam to Trump Rallies where they pay to wait for hours on end, to see their hero and listen to his sometimes nonsensical musings dappled with falsehoods and tangents. It doesn't matter if Trump's words don't always make sense or if he tries to cut Medicare, Planned Parent Hood (affordable womens care) and Food Stamps (SNAP) for the poor. It doesn't matter if Trump sides with Putin over US Intel and creates national security risks. Nor does it matter if Trump opens up National Park lands for drilling and fracking and lifts pollution regulations—He's their man!

Law Enforcement is encouraged to "maybe bash their heads on the car door" and "don't be so gentle with them" when making arrests. Many members of Law Enforcement are Trump Supporters and that number is increasing. People within the Trump Administration are witness to acts and behaviors that are unacceptable to them. When those people resign or are fired, it creates a moral emptiness that is fulled with eager Trump loyalists and sycophants.   clw

FUN FACT

A lot of this propaganda paraphernalia were made in China including the MAGA hats, flags and signs.

Hail to the Chef Salad

Ingredients

- 2 C Shredded Lettuce
- 4 oz Shredded Cheese
- 4 oz Ham, diced
- 4 oz Turkey, diced
- 1 oz Bacon Bits
- 1 Eggs, hard boiled, sliced
- 1 Avocado, diced
- 6 Cherry Tomatoes
- 1 Ccucumber, sliced
- Salad Dressing of your choice

Hail to the Chef Salad!!!

Directions

Arrange the lettuce, cheese, meats, eggs, and avocado however you like, add the dressing and salute your supreme salad whichever way you like.

'Resisters' feel powerless and frustrated as they watch the world around them change into a lawless dystopian crime scene. More hate crimes, vandalism, poverty, pollution and homelessness, opioid deaths and mass shootings, "kids in cold cages'—In their opinion, this is not what America is supposed to be about.

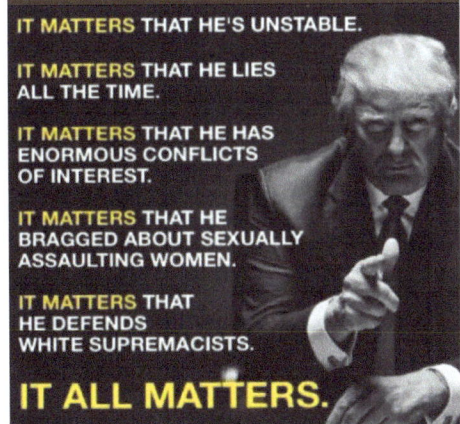

Republicans, support Trump through all the of the scandals and turmoil. He has given huge tax breaks to the very wealthy/corporations, repealed banking/corporate regulations and EPA standards. He is helping the oil & coal industry and ignoring green energy tech development. = More Winning!

Democrats are very annoyed, angry, sickened, disgusted and saddened to see the American ideals being destroyed. But mostly tired of what they see as a degradation of democracy and moral standards.

AK-47 Apple Pie

A teen allegedly wanted to 'shoot 400 people for fun.' Cops found an AK-47 in her bedroom.

BY KATIE SHEPHERD
SEPTEMBER 17 AT 10:08 AM

Alexis Wilson was working an afternoon shift at the local Pizza Inn in McAlester, Okla., on Sunday, when she pulled a co-worker aside to boast about her new gun.

politics
House passes bill loosening gun restrictions

Deirdre Walsh, CNN Senior Congressional Producer

Updated 8:40 PM EST December 6, 2017

VANITY FAIR
"Coincidence Number 395": The N.R.A. Spent $30 Million to Elect Trump. Was It Russian Money?

POLITICS
HUFFPOST
Paul Ryan Defends His Call For Prayers After Texas Mass Shooting: 'Prayer Works'

Mass shootings rates continue to rise

Mitch McConnell SOLD the Senate to the NRA for $1.26M.

He will NOT pass gun reform laws that 97% of Americans want, no matter how many DIE.

Vote him OUT, there's blood on his hands.

#DitchMitch
#MassacreMitch
#NRABloodMoney
#RebelResisters

AK-47 - Wikipedia
https://en.wikipedia.org › wiki › AK-47
The **AK-47**, officially known as the Avtomat Kalashnikova is a gas-operated, 7.62 ×39mm assault rifle, developed in the Soviet Union by Mikhail Kalashnikov.

300+ Mass Shootings in the US in 2019 Alone

FUN FACT
Convicted US felon arrested with more than 500 guns in California home

As #MassacreMitch Trends After Texas Shooting, Democrats Urge Mc...
Democratic leaders are pushing the Senate majority leader to take action on gun control legislation. "Enough is enough," House Speaker ...
huffpost.com

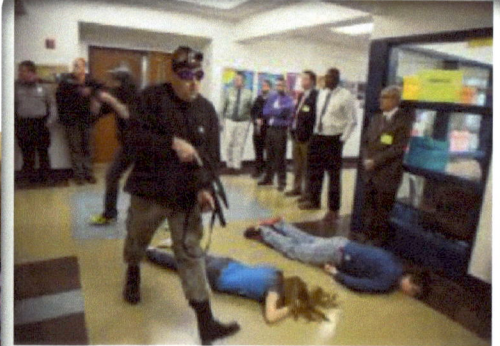

Schools Stage Active Shooter Drills
nbcnews.com

US felon caught with more than 500 guns

FUN FACT
HUFFPOST
After Texas Massacre, The State's Attorney General Calls For More Guns At Church

CNN
Texas church shooting leaves 26 dead, including 8 members of one family

"Good Guys With Guns"

(several patrons were actually armed at the time)

AK-47 Apple Pie

Ingredients

6 Apples
Pie Crust

Cinnamon
Cloves
Sugar

Directions

Feel safe with the AK-47 Apple Pie. Maybe you will feel so good and safe, you won't need that AK-47 after all.

Mix graham cracker crumbs, sugar, melted butter or margarine, and cinnamon until well blended. Press mixture into an 8 or 9 inch pie plate. Lay in apple and cinnamon mixture to cover pie crust. Bake at 375 degrees for 1 hour. Top with a big scoop of vanilla ice cream.

CBS News @CBSN... · 17h
Texas Department of Public Safety Regional Director Jeoff Williams on the White Settlement church shooting: "Unfortunately, this country has seen so many of these that we've actually gotten used to it at this point." cbsnews.com/news/west-free...

SAD FACT

SA Scientific American @sciam

More guns do not stop more crimes, evidence shows. Why do so many Americans believe the opposite? bit.ly/2IfaJrG

📌 This was one of our most important stories in 2017.

Sandy Hook Mom Slams Trump For Partying With NRA Head On Massacre Anniversary
"While they ignorantly partied and remained uninformed on an issue that kills thousands of Americans every year, I was crying myself to sleep."

Erica Buist @ericabuist

Why not just ban guns and when people are upset about it, just send them thoughts and prayers?

11/5/17, 2:07 PM

Loren F @citizenx1320 · Aug 23
Replying to @MusingMsAnthrop and @SenFeinstein
A knife is a mass murder weapon too. What's your plan to combat knife violence once you've destroyed the #2a ?

Republicans don't want stricter gun laws or background checks and they do not want restrictions for gun magazine size or high-powered automatic assault weapons. The GOP continues to block new gun laws.

Democrats want stricter gun laws and background checks and do not want automatic weapons or large ammunition magazines to be available to the public but they are not opposed to the 2nd Amendment.

Russian Roast

NBC NEWS

"Trump is on our side," says Russia-based asbestos maker ...
https://qz.com › trump-is-on-our-side-says-russia-based-asbestos-maker ▾
Apr 7, 2019 - Uralasbest believes the US president's commitment to deregulation is good news for makers of **asbestos**, a substance banned as a killer by ...

Putin praises Trump, says collusion claims are 'invented'

Prosecutors say longtime Manafort colleague has 'ties' to Russian intelligence

BY ROSALIND S. HELDERMAN AND SPENCER S. HSU
DECEMBER 4 AT 9:32 PM

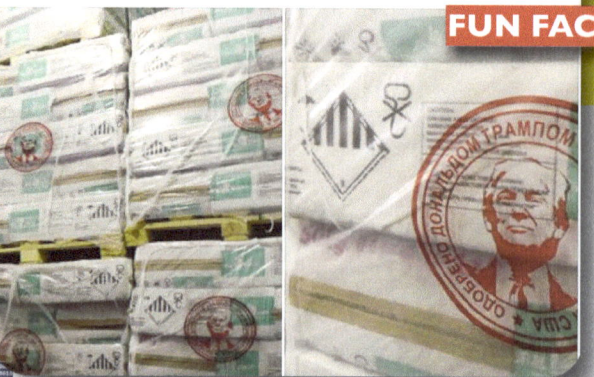

хризотил-асбеста.
Он поддержал руководителя Агентства по защите окружающей среды США Скотта Прюитта, который заявил, что его ведомство больше не будет занимат... See More

FUN FACT

The New York Times
Trump Pressed Top Republicans to End Senate Russia Inquiry

TOP STORIES

Reuters Top News
@Reuters

Russian company seeks to dismiss U.S. charges brought by Mueller reut.rs/2KiXil3

CBSNEWS
Experts say Russia hasn't stopped cyberattacks on U.S.

The Observer
Fake news and botnets: how Russia weaponised the web

6/25/18, 7:20 PM

CNN
Trump knew in January that Flynn misled FBI

POPULAR SCIENCE
Menu | Log In

The current theory is that the blast, which killed five scientists and blanketed the immediate region with a still-unknown amount of radiation, most likely involved a missile equipped with a miniature nuclear reactor.

WORLD NEWS
12/28/2017 08:23 AM EST

Russia Warns U.S.: Don't 'Meddle' In Upcoming Presidential Election

Vladimir Putin's government accused the U.S. of "direct interference" after the State Department urged the country to "hold genuine elections."

By Dominique Mosbergen

Jake Tapper ✓ @jaketapper · 51m
Let's be generous and assume this person hasn't followed the news and is unaware DOJ indicted a troll farm from Russia.

google.com/amp/s/www.wash...

Jack Posobiec ✓ @JackPosobiec · 4h
Apparently @JakeTapper thinks all Trump supporters are an "army of trolls" twitter.com/TrumpPatriotPL...

Russian Roast

Ingredients

1 Pork Roast
Olive Oil

Pepper
Salt

Note: This roast goes well with Mueller Marinade

Directions

Wash roast making sure to remove most nuclear residue if any. Place in baking pan or glass dish. Coat with oil and sprinkle with seasonings. Cover with **aluminum** foil to ensure ties with Russia's aluminum deal. Roast for 45 minutest to an hour depending on how much the radiation already cooked it.

Courier Journal
Braidy Industries is the Trojan horse that allows Russia to infiltrate Kentucky and the US

cleveland.com
'Moscow Mitch' gets a Russian-backed aluminum plant for Kentucky, but at what price? Letter to the Editor
We heard recently how Senate Majority Leader Mitch McConnell got himself a new aluminum plant for his state. Mitch, what was the price you ...

Politics | Reuters
Trump, Putin held a second, undisclosed meeting at G20 summit
U.S. President Donald Trump and Russian President Vladimir Putin held a second, previously undisclosed conversation during a dinner for G20 leaders at a summit...

Trump met with Putin twice, White House reveals
KTRK - Houston

Vladimir Putin's opening gambit in the new Great Game outfoxes Donald...
Business Standard India

Donald Trump Believed Vladimir Putin over U.S. Intelligence ...
https://www.newsweek.com › World › Donald Trump › International Affairs ▾
Feb 15, 2019 - Donald **Trump Believed** Vladimir **Putin** over U.S. Intelligence, Said North Korea Isn't a Threat Because Russian President Said So: McCabe ...

While most Americans cringed while watching the summit, Russians were very happy with the results

FUN FACT

npr
'Better Than Super': Russia Reacts To Trump-Putin Summit In Helsinki

Republicans don't seem to have a problem with Russian influence in the past, present or future elections and United States government.

Democrats believe Trump has had extensive communications and dealings with Russian oligarchs. Many believe Trump owes Russia and has compromised the highest level of office for personal gain.

PsychoGraphics Sushi

Data Mining • Algorithyms • Misinformation • Weaponized Psychographics Video Alts

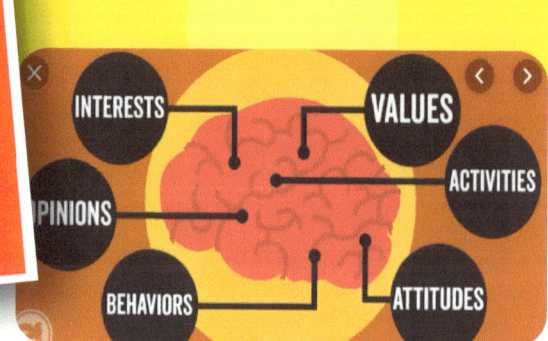

psy·cho·graph·ics
/ˌsīkōˈgrafiks/
noun

the study and classification of people according to their attitudes, aspirations, and other psychological criteria, especially in market research.

"Targeted Persuadables" Believed, 'Shared' and 'Retweeted' Fabricated, False Information That Stoked the Destructive Fires of Misinformation

Democrats had a hard time understanding why Republicans hated Hillary Clinton so much and thought she should be locked up. Democrats were not targeted like the Republicans were and did not see, or hear the conspiracy stories that were constantly being fed to the Republicans via algorithm targeting. The propaganda was made to look like the ads came from legitimate news sources. **The Trump campaign paid over one million dollars a day to Cambridge Analytica for their services.** clw

FUN FACT

Bannon actually came up with the name Cambridge Analytica

Republican "Persuadables" were "bombarded" with "Killery" type ads loaded with fabricated, negative imagery and content designed to invoke and incite rage against candidate Clinton.
Cambridge Analytica/The Great Hack

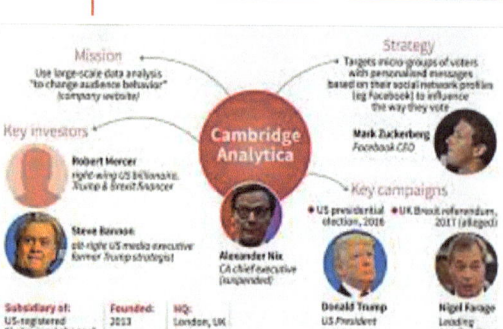

Cambridge Analytica ...

40

PsychoGrahics Sushi

Ingredients

Sushi : Avocado Slices

Psychographic Sushi ... Can you trust it....
I think so, but better ya never know.

Directions

Don't try this on your own. Get your info, I mean sushi from a tried and true source.
Don't mess around with this stuff. Could be very toxic if you are particularly susceptible

Some Examples of Propaganda

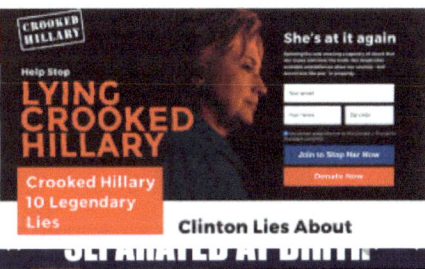

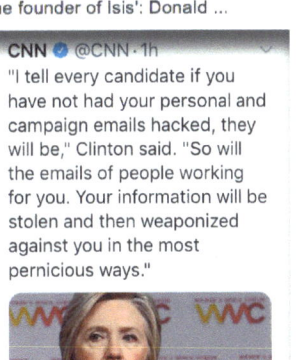

- Republicans may have heard that Russia influenced the election but few know how. Most Republicans have not even heard of Cambridge Analytica or the documentary called, The Great Hack, that details an operation targeting voters in 'Swing States.'
- Democrats were essentially 'left out of the loop' as they could recognize most false information and did not take the bait and 'share' or 'retweet,' therefore Russian scammers couldn't make $$. Also Democratic candidates did not partake of the propaganda targeting from companies like Cambridge Analytica.

EPA Muck Stew

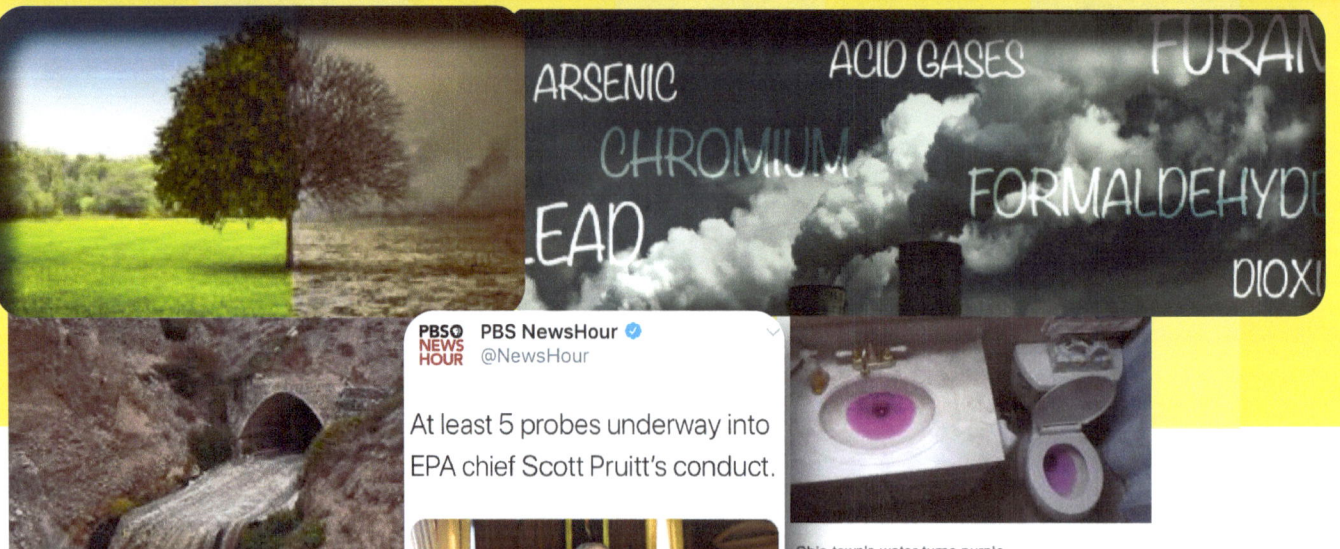

Ohio town's water turns purple ...
local12.com

Extreme water pollution threatens U.S

At least 5 probes underway into EPA chief Scott Pruitt's conduct
pbs.org

late changes to fracking study downplay ...
marketplace.org   Coal Grove Ohio

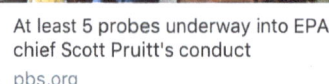

Flint's water crisis: what went wrong ...
theguardian.com

Was It 'Illegal' For Trump To Shrink Utah's Monuments? The Battle Begins

"WATER IS LIFE"

Trump plans to cut 2 million acres of national monument lands: report tandl.me/2AST7vu

Patagonia vows to sue Trump over national monuments
DEC 5, 2017 6:37 PM EST
BY RACHEL LAYNE / MONEYWATCH

Native American Tribes Join to File Lawsuit Against Trump Attack on Bears Ears National Monument

More pollution and less regulation and over-sight pose a threat to health and well-fare. Repercussions of poison air and water will be devastating and long-lasting

Republicans score another victory with the rolling back of Obama era EPA standards and regulations. The Trump Administration repeals the Clean Air Act and lessens regulation/over-sight for corporate air and water pollution.

42

EPA Muck Stew

Ingredients

- 2 lbs Beef trimmed, cubed
- 3 Tbsp Flour
- 1/2 tsp Garlic Powder
- 3 Tbsp Olive Oil
- 1 Onion, chopped
- 1/2 C Red Wine, optional
- 6 C Beef Broth
- 3 Tbsp Tomato Paste
- 1 tsp Rosemary
- 3 Potatoes, cubed
- 3 Carrots, pieces
- 1 C Peas
- 2 Tbsp Cornstarch
- 1 can Tomato Sauce
- 1 can Diced Tomatoes

Let it all simmer and fester until its nice and tender and mucky

Directions

Heat meat and olive oil in a large Crock Pot on HIGH until browned. Add red wine and beef stock, cook another 60 mins. Stir in all remaining ingredients except for peas, cornstarch and water. Reduce heat to medium low, cover and simmer 1 hour or until beef is tender (up to 90 minutes).

Mix equal parts cornstarch and water to create a muck. Slowly add the muck to the boiling stew until it reaches the desired consistency. Stir in peas and simmer for 5-10 more minutes before serving.

Oct. 11, 2019, 4:09 AM MDT
By Phil McCausland

Nearly one year ago, the Trump administration fired a panel of more than two dozen scientific experts who assisted the Environmental Protection Agency in its review of air quality standards for particulate matter.

The Obama administration averaged more than 18,000 EPA inspections related to the Clean Air Act, the Clean Water Act
That inspection figure has fallen to about 10,500.

Report: Trump to Announce Massive EPA Cuts

FUN FACT

The President Sold The Largest Amount Of Public Land In History, & It Will Affect Your Kids

On Monday, Trump will announce major cuts to the Environmental Protection Agency as he starts to build the budget for the next fiscal year, according to reports from Axios and the New York Times. A top official reportedly told Axios

Republicans win again with the repeal of Obama Environmental Protection (EPA) standards and regulations. for pollution control.

Democrats want more clean air and pollution regulations (not less). They also feel that minimizing air pollution can also help to stave off the repercussions of global warming and climate change.

Pigs-In-A-Blanket

"There is nobody better than a good cop. There is nobody worse than a bad cop."

Graphic video shows Daniel Shaver sobbing and begging officer for his life before 2016 shooting

Opinion: Trump's law enforcement policies are a welcome improvement from Obama's

Ron Hosko | FoxNews.com
Published on December 25, 2017

Dave McKenna @djmcke... · 1d
It is possible to take people into custody alive. That's what I keep telling myself. Fear or no fear, it is possible to not kill suspects.
💬 23   🔁 67   ♡ 571

James @delittletings · 1d
It is astonishing that the people of the United States allow themselves to be subject to summary execution by those they pay and trust to protect them, their fellow countrymen, whilst proclaiming their freedom and calling themselves proud

Holly Figueroa O'Reilly @AynRandPaulRyan · 7h
She was 28 years old.
She was playing video games with her 8-year-old nephew in her own home.
She was INSIDE THE HOUSE.

Repeat: she. was. inside. her. house. when. they. shot. her.
Say her fucking name because this shit has gone on FAR too long.
#TayJefferson #AtatianaJefferson

SHOT DEAD

Police fatally shot woman through a window while she and her nephew were playing video games

'To Serve and Protect'...

Whatever man those dogs are EXPERTLY trained before they reach the field. They move at the officers beck & call smh they ALLOWED that dog to chew on that HUMAN BEING for x amount of minutes and it's SICKENING and DISHEARTENING

Rhonda 10 minutes ago
Did you even watch the video? The guy was subdued. There was NO reason whatsoever for him to be punched in the head - multiple times at that. He was even trying to protect his face from the blows. It is astounding to me that the video did not disturb you at all. Same goes with some other posters here. I am not a liberal at all, but you have to be willing to call police brutality when it is obvious, like this video shows. Shame on you.

Police shot an innocent 62-year-old man in his own home, and bodycam footage refutes their story about why it happened

FOX NEWS
Cop who shot dead unarmed 17-year-old boy was sworn in just 90 minutes before,

Policeman punches young woman in the head on the Jersey Shore

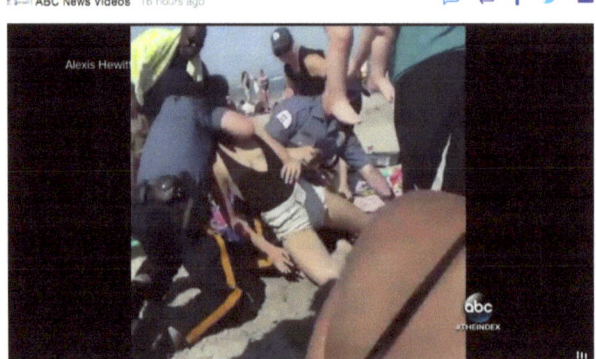

*You motherf*cker. Why did you do that?*

Pigs-In-A-Blanket

Ingredients

- 1 Package of Hot Dogs
- Pillsbury Crescent Roll or pie crust mix
- Mustard gas Sauce
- Spicy BBQ Sauce
- Relish

Enjoy this delicious snack from volume 1. This topic requires another serving.

Directions

Cut dough into triangle shapes or thin (1/2 inch) strips.
Put the hotdog on the widest side of the triangle and roll the hotdog and dough. Press to bind the dough in place. Place the pigs in a blanket on cookie sheet (not touching each other and bake at 350° for 20 minutes or until the dough is golden and flaky.

ROBO COP

Bots would be safer than "scared" cops who shoot to kill.

Thorough investigations, heavy fines and jail time for all of those operating above the law, should be standard procedure. Law Enforcement MUST BE HELD ACCOUNTABLE for violations against citizens. Higher diversity ratios within the force, along with surveillance camera & audio should also be standard procedure.

BEATEN BLIND

He complied peacefully for mug shot, then was handcuffed and taken to a room without cameras

IF YOU DON'T UNDERSTAND WHY COLIN KAEPERNICK KNELT DOWN FOR POLICE ACCOUNTABILITY IN THIS COUNTRY THIS IS WHY

#PhilandoCastile = No Conviction
#TerenceCrutcher = No Conviction
#SandraBland = No Conviction
#EricGarner = No Conviction
#MikeBrown = No Conviction
#RekiaBoyd = No Conviction
#SeanBell = No Conviction

Republicans think cops won't stop you, if you are not doing anything wrong and fatally shooting an unarmed person is OK if the officers were "scared."

Democrats believe there is a problem with police brutality cases (especially towards people of color) but realize the difficulties of law enforcement. No one should be allowed to operate above the law.

Hurricane Ham & Cheese

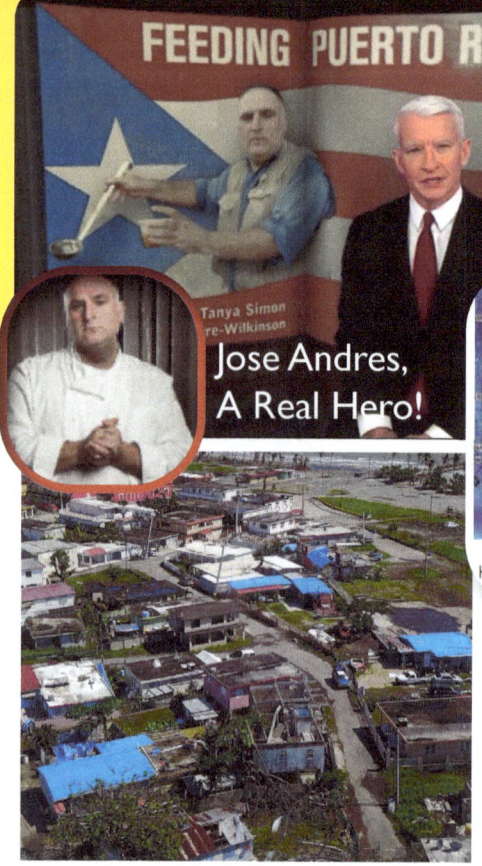

Private Citizens, and Celebrities Pitch In To Help Devastated Communities

Jose Andres, A Real Hero!

REAL HEROES
Private Citizens Like Chef Jose Andres, Pitch In To Help Fill The Gaps That FEMA Left Open.

FUN FACT

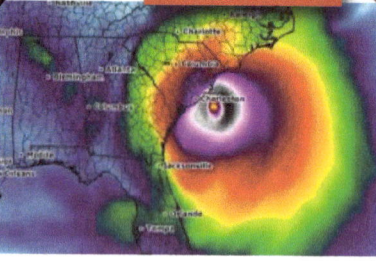

Maria
Irma
Harvey
Florence
Dorian

Major Hurricanes Are Becoming More Intense and More Frequent
Insurance Companies feel the strain even though many people didn't have separate flood insurance... and its going to get worse.

No power and growing anger at ground zero in Puerto Rico

52 Percent Of Harvey Victims Say Their FEMA Application Was Denied Or Is Still Pending

Many Texans say they're still "not getting the help" they need in the aftermath of the disaster, according to a new survey.

By Dominique Mosbergen

R The Root
Trump Administration Diverts FEMA Disaster Relief Money to Keep More Migrants in Cages
Trump Administration Diverts FEMA Disaster Relief Money to Keep More ... the federal government hostage over funding for his border wall.

E Earther
@EARTH3R

Puerto Ricans are spending the holidays in the dark trib.al/eYtYJj4

As Natural Disasters Increase, Trump Reduces Funding For FEMA

President Trump says he's "not sure that (he's) ever even heard of a Category 5" hurricane, despite four such storms having threatened the US since he took office

FUN FACT

Trump Defends His Golf Habit In Angry Tweet At London Mayor
Mayor Sadiq Khan quipped that the U.S. president was "clearly busy dealing with a hurricane out on the golf course."

46

12/28/17, 2:45 PM

Hurricane Ham & Cheese

Ingredients

2 slices Bread
4 slices Ham (Smoked or Reg.)
2 slices Cheese
(American, Swiss or Cheddar)

1 tsp. Margarine or
Coconut Oil

Doing the right thing can taste so good!

Directions

Fill bread slices with ham and cheese. Spread outsides of sandwiches with butter.
Cook in skillet on medium heat 3 min. on each side or until lightly browned on both sides.

Hurricane Dorian: Path of destruction ...
bbc.com

Rep. Jim McGovern ✔ @RepMcGovern · 19h
According to his own staff, Trump canceled his trip to Poland commemorating the start of World War II so he could "monitor the hurricane and our efforts to respond to it from the White House."

What did he do instead? He went golfing. Twice.

Video appears to show Trump golfing in Virginia in the run-up to catas...
Trump traveled to Camp David over the weekend. Pool reports said Trump made a stop at his golf course and video appears to show him ...

abcNEWS
Trump to appear via video as 5 former presidents gather for hurricane relief concert

WH🤮💩
@RPottery

I live on the coast of NC where we got pummeled by Dorian. Trump hasn't lifted a finger to help us. Most of the folks here are MAGAt's. I guess they might get the hint this time. At least I heard em grumbling about the fat orange blob #noFEMA #NCfuckedbyTrump #weneedhelp

9:28 AM · Sep 14, 2019 · Twitter for iPhone

 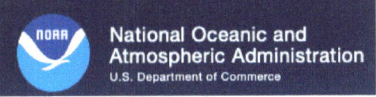

FEMA Mission Statement
Helping people before, during, and after disasters

Republicans send "Thoughts and Prayers." while diverting some of FEMA (disaster relief) funding to 'Build the Wall.' Houston, Puerto Rico, The Bahamas and many other areas remain devastated.

Democrats believe hurricanes and other natural disasters will become more prevalent due to the effects of climate change. They prefer to have more $$$ for disaster relief and preparedness as opposed to military spending and tax breaks for wealthy corporations.

Entitled & Emboldened Chicken Bratwurst

How should America talk about the Nazis next door?

Emmett Till, A 14 Year Old Boy was Brutally murdered by a Group of Men for Talking to a White Woman. His Face was Unrecognizable after beating

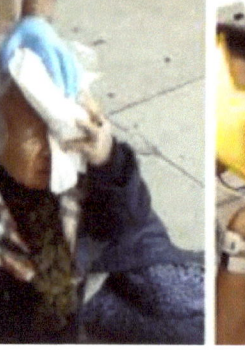

20 hours ago
Transgender Woman Found Burned Beyond ...
nytimes.com

Just in case some of you dont know, the Governor of Mississippi, Phil Bryant, is the nephew of Carolyn Bryant, the woman who lied that led to the death of Emmett Till and Roy Bryant who murdered Emmett Till.

The Untold Story of Emmett Louis Till – 14 year old tortured to death
By Geno 7 years ago

Reviewed by Melissa Antoinette Garza

There are times when something hits you so hard that the thought of it makes your heart pound harder and sadder and in a devastating way. Hearing about Emmett Till brings tears to my eyes and cast doubts in the conscience of humanity. Till was a young boy who was the victim of a vicious, unforgivable and despicable action. He was tortured and killed by racist

 ABC News @ABC · 33m
A white Mississippi woman accused of brandishing a handgun at an African American couple while telling them to leave a campground has been convicted of a misdemeanor and fined $250.

Straight couple savagely attacks gay ...
lgbtqnation.com

Asian Americans Are Targeted For Hate .
nextshark.com

$250 fine for white woman who brandished gun at black couple
A white Mississippi woman accused of brandishing a handgun at an African American couple while telling them to leave a campground has...
abcnews.go.com

♡ 136   ⟲ 101   ♥ 246

Anti-Asian Hate Crimes on the Rise · Tell Us How UC It: A ...
https://library.ucsd.edu › tellushowucit › items › show ▾
Often, school authorities manage to cover up alarming events such as violent hate crimes before members of college and university communities realize what ...

MusingsofaMisanthrope @MusingMsAnthrop · 2m
So the Mississippi governor is a relative of the people who brutally murdered the little boy?

Majority Of White Americans Think They're Discriminated Against

 Dolores Dace @Da
FUN FACT
I'm told the best way WP can change in a helpful way is 2speak out when we see racism, privilege, false equivalencies. 2 join, yet not lead.

♡ 11   ⟲ 12   ♥ 167

S.B. Stewart-Laing @... · 14h
Bingo! We didn't cause previous generations' messes but we all have a choice as to whether we pitch in to clean it up or make the problem worse.

NowThis @nowthisnews · 30m
This Black mother wearing a hijab was told to 'go back where you came from' at an amusement park — the same phrase used by Trump in reference to congresswomen of color

This is horrible.
1:35 23.9K views

Catholic priest says sorry for KKK cross burning on black couple's lawn

The Rev William Aitcheson tells Philip and Barbara Butler he was 'blinded by hate and ignorance' when he targeted them in 1977 at their home in Maryland

Entitled & Emboldened Chicken Bratwurst

Ingredients

Chicken Bratwurst : Lard

Sizzle up a few chicken brats always in a group, never alone when the cooking begins

Directions

Place the chicken bratwurst in a well oiled frying pan and cook on high heat until it pops.

Suspect arrested for throwing acid on Milwaukee man in alleged hate crime
Data collected by the FBI showed a 17% increase in hate crimes across the U.S. in 2017, the third annual increase in a row. Anti-Hispanic ...

NowThis @nowthisnews
A man in a MAGA hat sprayed protesters with bear repellant after a pro-impeachment march in Santa Monica

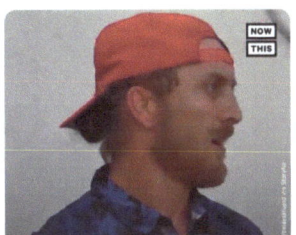

AP Oddities @AP_Oddities · 9m
Police say a North Carolina man wasn't just caught driving drunk. He also complained that an officer wouldn't share a bottle of liquor that was confiscated from someone else. apne.ws/L8Pwh7b #odd

Man Suspected Of Killing 3 Asians With Hammer Charged ...
https://www.huffpost.com › entry › asian-hammer-murders-brooklyn-hate-...
Feb 1, 2019 - Arthur Martunovich allegedly targeted the Asian restaurant workers at the Seaport ... Of Killing 3 Asians With Hammer Charged With Hate Crime.

USA TODAY
What we know: Woman admits to hitting teenage girl with car because girl was 'a Mexican'

Republicans felt they were "left behind," forgotten about and saw Donald Trump as their savior. They identify with Trump's alleged racist, xenophobic or homophobic ways. They applaud his violent rhetoric at rallies and feel emboldened.

Democrats are horrified at the discriminatory, violent, racist, homophobic and xenophobic behavior. They urge Trump to stop encouraging name-calling, violence and police brutality.

Foe Fried Rice

The New York Times
After Trump calls off talks, Afghanistan braces for violence
4h ago

North Korea testing 'creative' weapons that could threaten US, experts say
CNN.com
16 hours ago

U.S. war games in Kim Jong Un's backyard trigger 'nuclear war' warning
Two dozen U.S. stealth jets were among hundreds of aircraft involved in war games intended as a show of strength to neighboring North Korea on Monday.
by Alexander Smith | NBC NEWS

  NPR @NPR

North Korea fires two short-range ...
telegraph.co.uk

Are YOU Feeling Safer? (asking for a friend)

Iran installing advanced nuclear centrifuges, says IAEA as nuclear deal with US threatens to come apart

The White House has publicly blamed North Korea for a ransomware attack in May that locked more than 300,000 computers in 150 countries.

WASHINGTON AND THE WORLD
Trump Says ISIS Is Defeated. Reality Says Otherwise.
The radicalized children of the Islamic State will threaten the world for generations to come unless the president changes course.
By CHARLES LISTER | March 18, 2019

 Fox News
Putin again threatens to develop previously banned missiles if US does
Vladimir Putin warned the U.S. once again this week that Russia would develop missiles previously banned under a landmark nuclear forces ...
3 days ago

Threat From Within: Domestic Terrorism is on the Rise

There have been more mass shootings than days this year

As of September 1, which was the 244th day of the year, there have been 283 mass shootings in the U.S., according to data from the nonprofit Gun Violence Archive (GVA), which tracks every mass shooting in the country. The GVA defines a mass shooting as any incident in which at least four people were shot, excluding the shooter.

The toll of 283 mass shootings includes several high-profile, mass casualty attacks, two of which happened within 24 hours of each other:

North Korea says war with the U.S. is inevitable
"We do not wish for a war but shall not hide from it," an

The "Make America Safe Again mantra doesn't seem to pan out as North Korea and Russia conduct missile launch tests while tensions rise between Trump and the Taliban...not to mention a rise in domestic terrorism from white nationalists.

Foe Fried Rice

Ingredients

- 1 Package of Quinoa Rice
- 1 Egg
- Bell Peppers (Green, Orange, Red)
- Onion
- Soy Sauce

As things heat up, enjoy the safe and colorful Foe Fried Rice

Directions

Heat Scramble egg, set aside. Dice veggies and toss into a well oiled non-stick frying pan. Heat on medium until slightly tender. Add in rice and quinoa packet, heat thoroughly then mix in egg any soy sauce to taste. Goes great with a Dystopian Daiquiri.

Business Insider

New details on Russia's mysterious missile disaster suggest a nuclear reactor blew up

An explosion at a Russian weapons testing site in August released radioactive isotopes that almost certainly came from a nuclear reactor, ...

Bolton: Trump's lack of effective policy on North Korea puts U.S. forces and allies at 'imminent' risk

5:38 PM EST December 23, 2019
Video 02:30

Chuck Schumer @SenSchumer · 1h
President @realDonaldTrump turned his back on the **Kurds**—our leading partner in the fight against ISIS

As Trump's former Secretary of Defense said: This could lead to a resurgent ISIS

He is making Americans less safe, undoing years of work to fight ISIS

Our Kurdish Allies Are Decimated and ISIS Prisoners Flee After Trump Withdraws US troops

North Korea missile test : NPR
https://www.npr.org › tags › north-korea-missile-test
North Korea Conducts 3rd **Missile Test** Since Last Week Amid Stalled Talks With

Republicans are OK with Kim Jun Un's missile testing and "love letters" to Trump. Trump believes Kim Jun Un loves him and that they have a "great relationship."

Democrats don't feel safe with North Korea's unapproved missile testing nor of Putin's cyber attacks, aggression towards Ukraine and pushing of boundaries. Domestic terrorism is very unsettling.

Me Too Tacos

Lawsuit Could Put Trump's Sexual Misconduct Accusers Back In Spotlight

December 5, 2017 · 9:38 PM ET

HANSI LO WANG

NBC NEWS

Women who have publicly accused Trump of harassment speak out

23+ Donald Trump sexual misconduct allegations - Wikipedia
https://en.wikipedia.org › wiki › Donald_Trump_sexual_misconduct_alleg...
Donald Trump, an American businessman and current president of the United States

Sexual Harassment especially, in the workplace is all too common. A glaring lack of professionalism and respect for personal boundaries, needs to be addressed and brought to light. Women struggle for equal pay and promotion while fending off unwanted advances. But sexual harassment is aimed at children and men as well, with the common denominator being, the abuser will have some sort of power over them such as physical strength, an employer, a teacher, a priest, a coach or family member.   clw

The "Me Too" movement enabled people to rise up and speak out against abusive behavior, instead of normally keeping silent.

USA Gymnastics sex abuse scandal
axios.com

FOX NEWS
Fox News host wonders if #MeToo is 'killing all the fun of Christmas'

Is #MeToo movement 'spoiling' Christmas? Fox Ne...
rt.com

♡ 21   ↻ 35   ♡ 33   ✉

Gail Parenti @ParentiGail · 2h
Oh man, you mean guys can't be all rapey and make their female coworkers uncomfortable at will? Where's the fun in that?

The Catholic Church routinely engaged in Pedophilia throughout the centuries. Countless abuses are systematically covered up by high ranking ordained members.

The movie *Spotlight* exposes their extensive cover-up system.

Pope Francis Removes the Secrecy Requirements for Church Documents on Child Sex Abuse

Activists have called for the move to help investigators gather evidence against offenders

  BBC News (World) ✓
@BBCWorld

Trump accused of 'slut shaming' Senator Kirsten Gillibrand

Trump accused of 'slut shaming' senator

Senate Democratic women call on Franken to resign amid further allegations of sexual harassment

Me Too Tacos

Ingredients

- Fish Fillet or Fish Sticks
- Tortillas
- Cabbage Mix
- South Western Chipotle Sauce

Acknowledge and respect the nutrients and flavor of these Me Too Tacos.

Directions

Fry, bake or broil the fish. Sprinkle tortilla with shredded cheese. Place cooked fish on top and then add shredded cabbage mixture. Drizzle sauce over top. Salt to taste.

allegations against Epstein ...
miamiherald.com

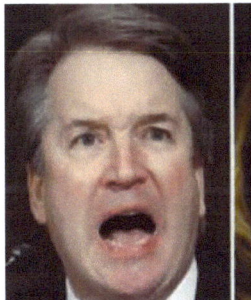 

Kavanaugh Hearings ...
Kavanaugh's very animated, hysterical refute was seen as unstable and unbecoming for a Supreme Court Justice

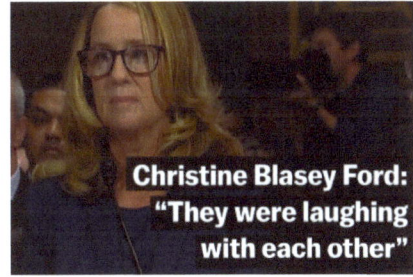

Christine Blasey Ford: "They were laughing with each other"

'He Grabbed Me There in the Front': Donald Trump Allegedly Hid Behind a Tapestry to Grope a Woman at Mar-a-Lago
4664 reactions   4%   68%   28%

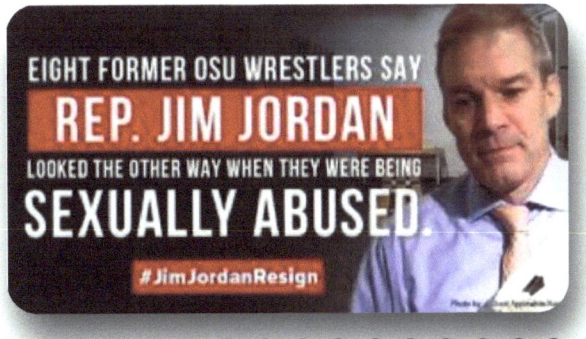

EIGHT FORMER OSU WRESTLERS SAY REP. JIM JORDAN LOOKED THE OTHER WAY WHEN THEY WERE BEING SEXUALLY ABUSED. #JimJordanResign

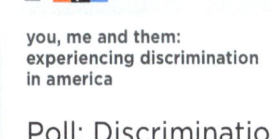

you, me and them: experiencing discrimination in america

Poll: Discrimination Against Women Is Common Across Races, Ethnicities,

- Republicans seem to be OK with sexual harassment and sexual assault. They over-look such accusations and continue to vote for and protect political officials who have been accused, while issuing insults and death threats to the victims who speak out.

- Democrats see sexual harassment as being unacceptable and amoral. They aim for higher standards, especially in public office. Democrat Al Franken resigned for making lewd gestures a decade ago.

Democrat Detachment Donut Holes

Democrats load "subpoena cann...
axios.com

@jefftiedrich

imagine being so fucking stupid that you look at this ignorant clown, this racist moron, this feeble-minded simpleton, this bloated nitwit with his cotton candy hair and radioactive tangerine skin and disheveled shapeless clothing and think "now here is a man to worship"

8:38 AM · 4/18/18 · Twitter Web Client

Stephanie Kennedy @WordswithSteph · 17h
Seriously, how many scandals can Donald Trump pack into one presidential term? This is exhausting. And seemingly endless. Please, I am imploring everyone to support Democratic candidates in any way you can. Trump and all his complicit enablers must be defeated.

🔁 ❤️IndigenousPeople❤️ Retweeted
 WH🇺🇸🧑‍🎨 @RPottery · 5h
I live on the coast of NC where we got pummeled by Dorian. Trump hasn't lifted a finger to help us. Most of the folks here are MAGAt's. I guess they might get the hint this time. At least I heard em grumbling about the fat orange blob #noFEMA #NCfuckedbyTrump #weneedhelp

HuffPost
Here Are The 81 People And Entities Close To Trump Democrats Are Investigating
The list includes Trump's sons, Eric Trump and Donald Trump Jr., as well ... current and former members of Trump's administration, inaugural committee ... some are expected to fight the request and force a possible
Mar 4, 2019

 Tina Marie 🌊🇺🇸 @tinamarief49 · 15h
Replying to @WordswithSteph
Every single day it's something else with Trump
He is exhausting
So sick of his bs
🌊

WTFGOP? #ImpeachmentIsComing @DogginTrump · 20h
My mother always told me not to use the word hate because hate is a strong word

So let me just say, I HATE this motherfucker with every fiber of my being

Mr. President, I Want Out of This Abusive Relationship
Co-Dependency, Enabling, Fear, and Cowardice in the Age of Trump

Democrat Detachment Donut Holes

Ingredients

1 can refrigerated Biscuits
butter, melted
1/4 C Sugar
1 tsp Cinnamon

1 C Powdered Sugar
2 tbsp Milk
1/4 tsp Vanilla Extract
Sprinkles

Life is just a bunch of crazy donut holes

Directions

For the cinnamon sugar mix, in a bowl, add 1/4 cup sugar and 1 teaspoon cinnamon and mix. For the vanilla glaze mix, in a bowl, add 1 cup powdered sugar, 2 tablespoons milk, and 1/4 teaspoon vanilla extract and mix. Separate the dough into 8 pieces. Slice each piece of dough into fourths. Roll these pieces into small balls. Place the balls into a large saucepan filled with oil, heated to 350°F. Fry for 1 minute. For the vanilla glaze mix, dip the donut holes into the glaze and top with sprinkles. For regular glazed donut holes, leave out the sprinkles. For the cinnamon sugar glaze, coat the donut holes in 2 tablespoons melted butter, then cover with the cinnamon sugar mixture.

The message, originally shared anonymously online a year ago, warns of what will happen when liberals regain control of the White House.

It includes a host of immortal lines.

We're going to tax your mega churches so bad Joel Olsteen will need to get a job at Chik Fil A to pay his light bill. Speaking of Chik Fil A, we're buying all those and giving them to any LGBTQ person your sick cult leaders tortured with conversion therapy.
Guns will apparently be a thing of the past.
We're going to gather up ALL of your guns, melt them down and turn them into a gargantuan metal mountain emblazoned with the face of Hillary Clinton.
Immigration will be welcomed, as per the words at the base of the Statue of Liberty.
Every single public school will be renamed after a child that was kidnapped by this regime.
And after we fumigate the WH, we're repainting the whole thing rainbow.

The conclusion of the diatribe is a work of art.
And every single time a Trumpster complains about any of the changes, we're adding an openly gay character to a Disney movie.

- Republicans think Democrats are "Whiny Snowflakes" and sore losers.

- Democrats are stunned at the glaring malicious and incompetent actions of the Trump Administration and some say, worse than that, are the Trump Supporters. Realizing "they are walking among us" has been a disturbing notion. They find themselves thinking and behaving in ways they never saw themselves.
There normal "PC Ways" are now more angry and (passive) aggressive. But Dems aren't street-fighters...yet.

Resignation Rigatoni

Kelly: 'I don't think I'm being fired ...
cnn.com

Trump lashes out at Rex Tillerson for ...
nbcnews.com

Reuters
President Donald Trump's aides and confidants are concerned about his mental state after days of erratic behavior and wild outbursts.

"His mood changes from one minute to the next based on some headline or tweet, and the next thing you know his entire schedule gets tossed out the window because he's losing his s---," one former White House official, who spoke on the condition of anonymity.

Attorney General Sessions fired over ...
pri.org

DECEMBER 29 20°

TOP STORIES

Chief of Staff John Kelly Fired Omarosa ...
eurweb.com

SEAN SPICER HAD A MELTDOWN AFTER TRUMP FIRED COMEY, HIDING IN BUSHES AND DEMANDING DARKNESS
BY JULIA GLUM ON 5/10/17 AT 11:35 AM EDT

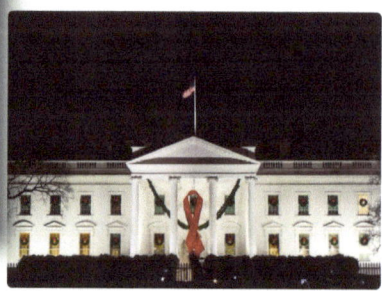
The Washington Post
Trump administration fires all members of HIV/AIDS advisory council `FUN FACT`

...ores becomes 5th Texas Congressman to not run for reelection
...xteen is the number of House Republicans retiring so far this year. And ...e is the number of those representatives from Texas alone. The list ...
msnbc.com

Politics The Independent
'Serving under Trump is embarrassing': Fifth Republican congressman retires in just two weeks as GOP fears more exits
A fifth Republican congressman appears set to quit the party in the space of two weeks amid ongoing tension over Donald Trump's presidency. Representative Mike Conaway will not seek re-election to his Texas seat in 2020, the Politico website reported. He has not confirmed his decision or reason for...

Trump now says he fired Mattis 2 months ...
businessinsider.com

Resignation Rigatoni

Ingredients

1 pkg Rigatoni
1/4 c Olive Oil
6 Garlic Clove crushed
1 red Chili Pepper, finely chopped

2 Courgettes
1 C Fresh Shredded Parmesan
1 tsp Lemon Juice

Freshly sliced basil

Enjoy Resignation Rigatoni while it lasts, it may be gone at a moments notice

Directions

Cook the pasta following the packet instructions. Drain, keeping back 2 tbsp of the cooking liquid. Heat 2 tbsp olive oil in a frying pan and add the garlic and chili and cook for a minute. Add the courgettes and fry for 5-6 minutes until softened. Stir through the lemon juice. Toss the pasta with mixture and garnish with basil before serving.

Over 56 High-Ranking Officials Have Left the White House under Trump
(as of 12/19)

FUN FACT

FBI Director
Secretary of State
National Security Advisor
White House Chief of Staff
Attorney General
EPA Administrator
Secretary of Defense

 Axios updated Nov 25, 2019

Director of Government Ethics
White House Chief Strategist
Communications Director
Secretary of Health & Human Services
Secretary of Veterans Affairs
FEMA Administrator
Labor Secretary
Director of National Security

...to name a few

Paul Ryan Struggles To Explain Why Trump Shouldn't Have To Resign Over Sexual Misconduct Claims

He said he's only focused on misconduct in Congress.

By Willa Frej

Axios

Andrew McCabe sues Justice Department over "politically motivated" firing

Former FBI Deputy Director Andrew McCabe is suing the Justice Department and the FBI for violating his First Amendment rights by firing him ...
Aug 8, 2019

Republican White House Staff has a very high rate of turnover. Some are out-right fired while others "resign." Many of the departures are unexpected, swift and are accompanied by public ridicule and disparaging words from Trump himself.

Democrats can only watch as life-long, high-ranking, bipartisan officials leave the Trump Administration one by one...leaving grossly unqualified, under-staffed and/or sycophant staffers.

Sautéed MisInformation Mushrooms

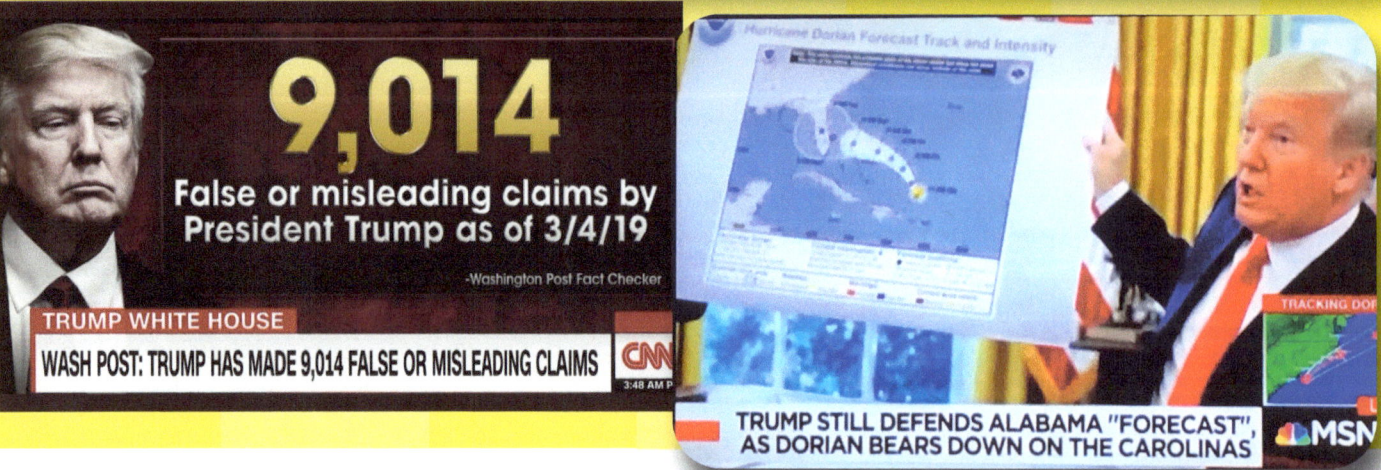

FAKE NEWS! "Enemy of the People" The First Amendment is being put to the test. Press briefings, daily news, twittter feeds & Wikileaks pour into the MSM arena with high volume and ferocity, though veracity is the main issue as real-time 'Fact-Checking' has become a necessity. Presidential rallies and press briefings are littered with miss-speak and bold-faced lies at times. Outrage from opposing parties and citizens grow with each day. "Mis-information" played a prominent roll in demonizing Hillary Clinton's Presidential Campaign and some would argue that the Comey briefing regarding her emails, held 10 days before the 2016 election, sealed her fate. Hillary Clinton underwent thorough investigation(s) and was cleared but the damage was done.   clw

Ex-Cambridge Analytica employee: If Trump wins in 2020, blame Facebook

BY BRITTANY KAISER

This week, Mark Zuckerberg made what appeared to be a big announcement: Facebook is implementing new measures to stop foreign actors from intervening in U.S. politics. From

Conway Is Famous For Her "Alternative Facts"

FEDERAL OFFICE RECOMMENDS KELLYANNE CONWAY BE REMOVED FOR REPEATED HATCH ACT VIOLATIONS

Congress explicitly refused to fund the president's border wall that Mexico was supposed to pay for. Now he is trying to divert billions of dollars anyway. Will lawmakers let him?

THIS IS THE PRESIDENT

Trump diverts money for schools to build wall
Congress explicitly refused to fund the president's border wall that Mexico was supposed to pay for. Now he is trying to divert billions of dollars anyway. Will ...
msnbc.com

Politics AFP
Netanyahu 'played' Trump with misinformation: Tillerson
Netanyahu Lost. His Enemies Won. But Who Can Govern Israel? The Daily Beast
Israel's Netanyahu Says He'll Seek to Form a 'Zionist' Government Without Arab Parties Meredith Videos

Donald J. Trump ✓
@realDonaldTrump

I often stated, "One way or the other, Mexico is going to pay for the Wall." This has never changed. Our new deal with Mexico (and Canada), the USMCA, is so much better than the old, very costly & anti-USA NAFTA deal, that just by the money we save, MEXICO IS PAYING FOR THE WALL!

♡ 112K   6:38 AM - Dec 13, 2018

The Washington Post ✓ @... ·3h
Fact Checker: Trump tops 12,000 false or misleading claims in under 950 days

"The Wall is Ahead of Schedule!"

Sautéed MisInformation Mushrooms

Ingredients

- 1 Pkg Broccoli & Cauliflower
- 1 Onion
- 1 Egg
- 1/2 C Panko/Bread Crumbs
- 1/2 C Flour
- 3 Tbsp Water
- Crushed Red Pepper
- Oil (for frying)
- Ponzu Sauce

So its just a different type of mushroom...You'll love it, TRUST ME. I know more about mushrooms than anyone.

Directions

Clean and cut mushrooms, set aside. Prepare flour and water mixture and a separate bowl or plate filled with Panko or bread crumbs. Submerge mushrooms into flour mixture and then roll each mushroom through Panko/bread crumbs coating completely. Preheat a frying pan with 1/4" of cooking oil on medium heat. Gently place coated mushrooms in oil and turn after a minute or so. When golden crispy, lift with slotted spoon. Serve with Ponzu.

USA TODAY
President Trump went to 'extraordinary lengths' to hide details of Putin meetings, report says
After meeting with Putin at the 2017 Group of 20 summit in Hamburg, ... from Trump's meetings with Putin and, after the 2018 Helsinki meeting, ...
In-Depth · Jan 13, 2019

PERSPECTIVE
It's time to take Fox News's destructive role seriously

Kellyanne introduces an "alternative Constitution".
Kellyanne Conway: It's unconstitutional for Democrats to 'embarrass this president' with impeachment -

Kellyanne Conway: It's unconstitutional for Democrats to 'embarrass this presi...
White House aide Kellyanne Conway on Sunday insisted that Democrats do not have a "constitutional basis" to embarrass President Donald Trump by ...
🔗 rawstory.com
11:12 AM · Sep 15, 2019 · Twitter Web Client

Misinformation is Detrimental to Our Democracy and Our National Security

•

Society Crumbles without Honesty and Integrity

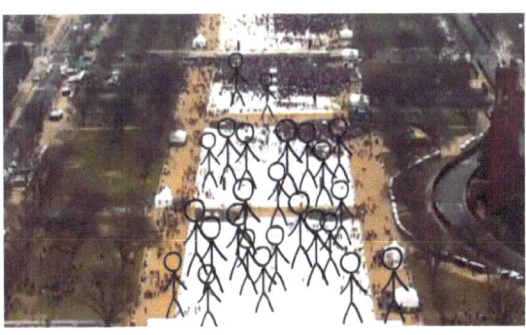

Adam Blickstein @AdamBlickstein · 6h
BREAKING: Trump releases new inauguration photo confirming massive crowd

Republicans are OK with Trump's chronic exaggerations, misleading and straight out lying. Trump Supporters are generally unaware of the magnitude and scale of misinformation aimed directly at them.

Democrats are aware of the dangers of malicious misinformation and are dismayed at the lack of 'calling out' of numerous falsehoods conveyed by the Trump Administration.

Sooper Elite Salad

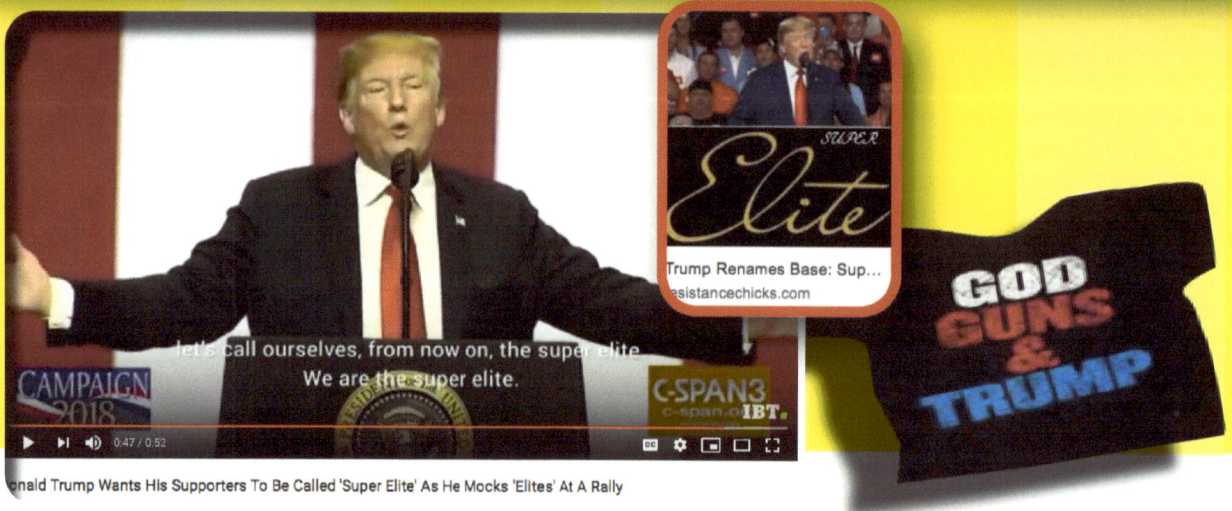

"[We have] more money, brains, better houses and nicer boats, hence... "Super Elite"

IBTimes UK
Published on Jun 28, 2018

President Donald Trump once again mocked the "elite" class during a campaign rally in Fargo, North Dakota on June 27, and suggested that his supporters be, hereafter, called the "super elite." He said he has got more money, brains, better houses, and nicer boats, hence the new label.

Nicki Lisa Cole, Ph.D.
Updated June 29, 2019
Many were shocked by Donald Trump's rise to prominence through the 2016 Republican primaries, and even more so by his win of the presidency. Simultaneously, many were thrilled by it. Who are the people behind Trump's success?

Big Picture
This set of facts, culled from a series of surveys conducted by one of the U.S.'s most respected public opinion research centers, leaves us with a clear picture of those behind Trump's rise to political prominence. They are primarily white, older men with low levels of education and income. They believe that immigrants and free trade deals have harmed their earning power (and they're right about the free trade deals), and they prefer an America in which white people are the majority. Trump's worldview and platform seem to resonate with them.

Yet, following the election, exit poll data shows that Trump's appeal was far broader than polling and voting during the primaries suggested. He captured the votes of the vast majority of white people, regardless of age, class, or gender. This racial division in the electorate further played out in the ten days following the election, when a surge of hate crimes, fueled by an embrace of Trump's rhetoric, swept the nation

The New York Times
With the Faithful at Trump's North Carolina Rally: 'He Speaks Like Me'
Two months after his rally there produced "send her back" chants, the president brought identity politics back to the state.
1 day ago

"I Love The Poorly Educated!"

(...and the Willfully Ignorant)

Sooper Elite Salad

Ingredients

- 1 C Baby Spinach
- 1 C Spring Mix
- 6 Hemp Seed Oil
- 1 Tbsp Red Onion, diced
- 1 Avocado, diced
- 1/4 Kalamata Olives
- Shredded Parmesan Cheese
- Hemp Seeds

If you are feeling "Sooper Elite" you should enjoy this 'high brow' salad..

Directions

Mix it all together and sprinkle as much fresh, shredded Parmesan cheese as you like, 'cause you're so 'Sooper!'

63% of Trump Supporters Are White Non-College
Pew Research Center

Trump's Super-Elite Populism - The Atlantic
theatlantic.com

Republicans have been viewed as being less educated (hicks) unaware of political facts and occurrences. They still chant, "Lock Her Up!" and demand HRC be investigated (even though she went through a Republican lead hearing and was found not guilty...BEFORE the 2016 election).

Democrats feel that most Republicans are ignorant of actual facts and lack the integrity and grace to carry on a meaningful conversation on political topics without resorting to lies and childish name-calling.

White Privilege Potatoes

VIDEO: WHITE WOMAN CALLS POLICE ON BLACK FAMILY'S BBQ FOR 'TRESPASSING' IN OAKLAND PARK

"BBQ Betty" has become a nickname for women who call Police to report innocent People of Color.

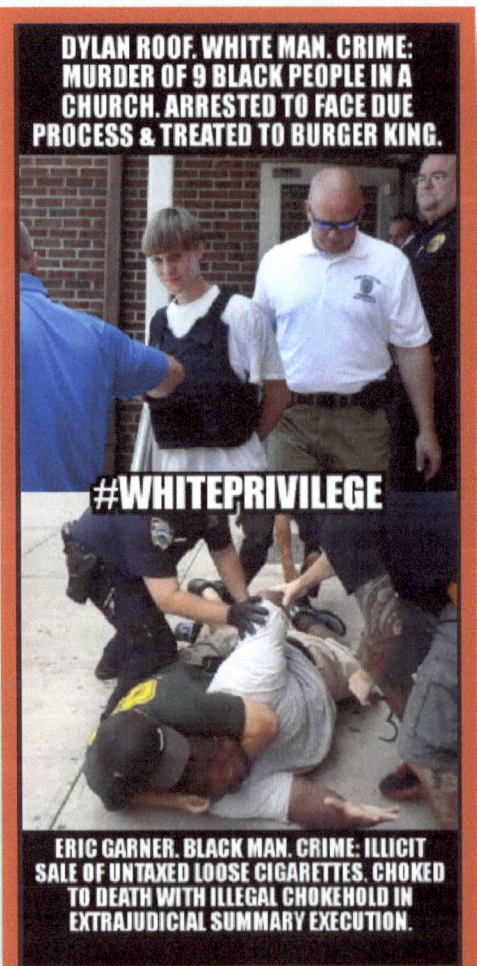

> White privilege **doesn't** mean your life hasn't been hard; it means that your skin color isn't one of the things making it **harder**.

A white man shot members of his own family then ran around, naked, strangling people. Cops never even drew their weapons while black kids are choked and shot for petty theft or selling cigarettes.

A Few White Privilege Examples:

1. Driving
2. Shopping
3. Eating Out
4. Applying for Jobs
5. Buying a Home/apt
6. Favors/Free Passes
7. Emergency/Medical Help
8. Having a Legal Gun in Public

Note: If this list means nothing to you, its a good chance you have no idea you are privileged compared to some other people. Are you strong enough to be black.

FUN FACT

The biggest number of Illegal immigrants are flooding into the US by way of over-staying their VISA. They are Europeans and Canadians but they are not rounded up and put into detention centers.

62   Are You Strong Enough To Be Black?

White Privilege Potatoes

Ingredients

6 White Potatoes
1 Cup White Milk
Salt
White Pepper
Butter

Directions

Indulge yourself with tasty White Privilege Mashed Potatoes. Eat as much as you like and don't even think about sharing with anyone else. Don't even bother cleaning up after yourself.

Peel off all brown skin from potatoes. Boil WHITE POTATOES ONLY until tender. Drain off most of the water. Mash and mix with white milk as needed to make a pasty white batch.
Add white salt and butter to taste.
…You could add hemp seed oil, black garlic, fresh green oregano leaves and pepper but that might be out of your comfort zone.

FUN FACT

Visa Overstays Far Exceed Illegal Border Crossings – Should Immigration Enforcement Focus on Visas, Not a Wall?

Instead of focusing on enforcement at the border, should the U.S. shift its focus to visa overstays?

These women were called out for wearing full KKK costumes on the streets of LA (via @iamshatown & @hiphopnational)

Republicans may not believe in, or admit to "white privilege" and the ones who do see it may believe they are simply the 'chosen ones' and feel they are entitled to special treatment above others.

Democrats are realizing the depth of racial injustices throughout society—more so now that racially motivated incidents have increased and come to light.

Trump Base Cheese Burger

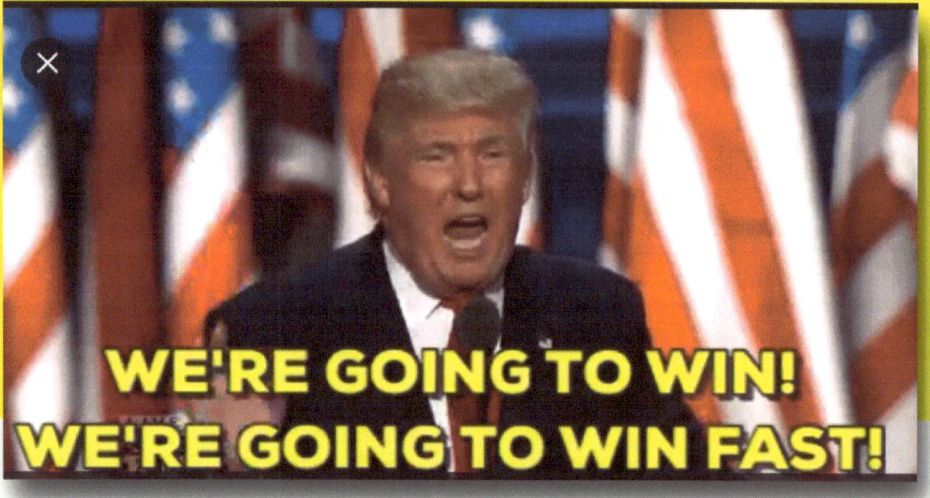

Trump voters see his flaws but stand by president who 'shakes things up'

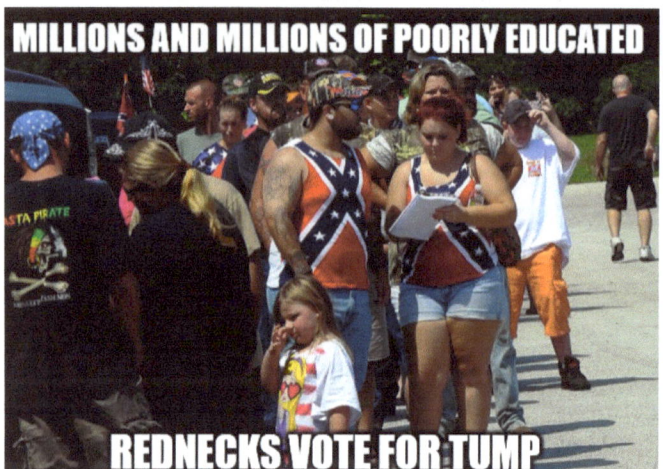

White House Fast Food Banquet

FUN FACT
The Trump Admin honors USA champion sports teams with a fast food banquet.

Generally, the Trump Base is mostly composed of the non-college, older white, rural, religious

The Guardian
@guardian

'We're under attack': young conservatives gather to reject political correctness

POLITICO
MAGAZINE

This Evangelical Leader Denounced Trump. Then the Death Threats Started.

Forget the Religious Right. Jen Hatmaker believes Christianity should stand for something different—and her hundreds of thousands of followers agree.

By Tiffany Stanley | Dec 17, 2017

Trump Base Cheese Burger

Ingredients

You know who has the ingredients for these things... Yes, you know who!

Now go out and get Trump's favorite food.

Nothin' but the best for his base!

Directions

No point in giving directions on how to make one of these when Trump's base knows you can get 'em just up the street, down around the corner, at that fast food joint.

U.S. The Daily Beast
Tomi Lahren: We Need Guns to 'Defend Ourselves' From Immigrants
Fox Nation host Tomi Lahren declared on Friday that Americans need guns in order to potentially fight off unlimited immigrants coming into the United...

Trump Supporter blocks Native American man

Trump supporters and Native American

Republicans don't care if Trump inherited his fortune and is a draft-dodger. They don't care if he has numerous bankruptcies and lawsuits against him. They don't care if he lies regularly and praises Putin. They believe they are "winning" with new tariffs, coal/oil production, less regulations and a "big beautiful border wall." (isn't actually built yet but took $3 BILLION from military, and FEMA)

Democrats are astounded at what they see as a lack of morals and foresight Republicans display. Democrats prefer green energy development, strict pollution control and wall street regulations, etc.

Comic Mac & Cheese

Mad Magazine (June, 2017) ...

Yes, MAD Magazine is still dishin' it.

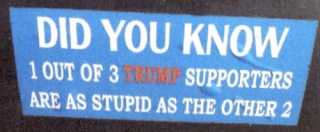

G7 FINAL COMMUNIQUE

Not bragging but my lawyer, Rudy talked my speeding ticket down to Manslaughter.

Trump, himself retweeted this photoshopped image on the left while "Libtards" quickly responded with a factual image.

Comic Mac & Cheese

Ingredients

- 1 Pkg Mac & Cheese
- 1/4 C Milk
- 1/4 Butter or Coconut Oil
- 1/2 C Shredded Cheese
- Garlic Powder
- Turmeric
- Fresh Shredded Parmesan
- Tri-Color Coarse Pepper

Directions

Enjoy this all-time kid favorite and reminisce about when comics were funny and politics were not.

Follow directions on the box, then add all the fun extras.

Late Night Talkshow Hosts Continue to Ride the Trump Gravy Train

Colbert, Kimmel, Meyers, Noah and even Falon, (who tries to remain neutral), blast out punchy one-liners and witty retorts to 'All Things Trump.'

Republicans stand by their fearless leader. He is their hero and most of them believe he is "Chosen by God" and/or the "Best President Ever." They do not like how badly the media treats their leader.

Democrats just watch as mesmerized Trump Supporters flock to rallies to hear mispronounced words, childish name-calling, broken tangents, exaggerations, ego-stroking and falsehoods. Dems rely on late night talkshow hosts for comic relief.

Tumpland Bites

Steve Silberman @stevesilberman · Oct 11
Now that it looks like Deutsche Bank disappeared Trump's tax returns and scrubbed its servers, it seems like an appropriate moment to mention that Trump's "special banker" at Deutsche was Justice Kennedy's son (not mentioned in this recent news).

Deutsche Bank may have destroyed copies of Trump's tax returns, cle...
The bank told a federal appeals court that it no longer holds records of President Donald Trump's tax returns.
newsweek.com

Donald Trump and PACs for Mitch McConnell, Marco Rubio, Scott Walker, and Lindsey Graham accepted $7.35mill in contributions from a Ukrainian-born oligarch who is the business partner of 2 of Vladimir Putin's favorite oligarchs & a Russian government bank.

NRA Is So Powerful and Why Gun Control ...
newsweek.com

Oil drilling in state parks ...
greenbang.com

Risk of Violence as Election Day Nears
nbcnews.com

"Our economy is the envy of the world. Perhaps the greatest economy we've had in the history of our country."

POLAR OPPOSITES

The country is divided with opinions that are polar opposites. What is considered "winning" by Republicans is losing for Democrats.

For Example: Republicans are OK with auto-assault rifles, increased oil & coal mining, **less** EPA regulations, huge tax cuts for the wealthy, **less** funding for community services and public education—the exact opposite of what Democrats want.

How the EPA's rollback of Obama-era environmental restrictions will impact climate

Trumpland Bites

Ingredients

- Chicken Bites
- Dipping Sauce

Enjoy Trumpland Bites with a nice Cult 45 Pale Ale!

Directions

Just Pick some up at that fast food joint...but don't forget the dipping sauce. They always forget the dipping sauce!!!

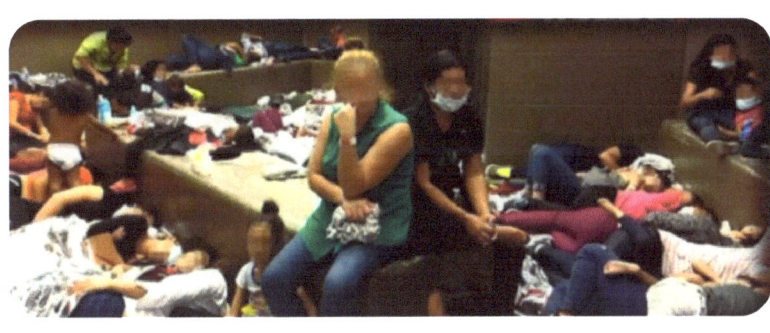

ICE RAIDS Pull Workers From Their Jobs and Kids From Schools

Opioid Crisis Leads to More Deaths

Republicans are winning with more oil fracking allowed on US Parks and coal mining. They praise police officers who are "extra tough" on suspects and applaud the dismantling of Obamacare. They are OK with using Military funding for the Border Wall instead of Mexico paying as promised. They believe huge tax cuts for the rich will 'trickle down' and they are OK with immigrant detention centers and ICE raids. Democrats want gun control, stronger EPA & FEMA funding (not less). They are appalled with ICE raids and the lack of proper care at detention centers.

Climate Change Chili

Trump: US could use some 'good old global warming' during cold snap on9news.tv/2DudxZ0

FUN FACT

USA TODAY
Paris withdrawal: Trump officially turns his back on climate crisis and our own children
Leaving the Paris climate agreement isn't about putting America first. ... Trump, who has called climate change a "hoax," likes to boast that, ...

Sierra Club @SierraClub · 27m
Methane is a greenhouse gas that's 87 times more potent than carbon dioxide when it's in the atmosphere & a public health risk. We must #CutMethane pollution now. TAKE ACTION: Tell your reps to support #HR2711 to protect us from methane pollution

Thick like sludge. For our health and the environment, we need to end the oil age.

Unprecedented devastation of ...
axios.com

Reuters Top News @Reuters · 9m
The world's northernmost town of Longyearbyen, in Norway's Svalbard archipelago, is struggling to cope with the effects of climate change, @alexnfraser reports reut.rs/32pbwtw

Deadly oil spill devastates Borneo port city – in pictures
theguardian.com

Climate change is cooking salmon in the Pacific Northwest
Warmer waters in the Pacific Northwest are killing salmon before they can reproduce.

President Trump says he's "not sure that (he's) ever even heard of a Category 5" hurricane, despite four such storms having threatened the US since he took office

SarcasticRover @Sarc... · 21m
What the flipping flip???!!! HOW DO YOU BAN THE WORD "SCIENCE-BASED"?!

David Beard @dabeard
CENSORSHIP—#Trump admin bans #CDC from using these words/phrases in budget docs:

-Fetus
-Transgender
-Diversity
-Vulnerable
-Science-based
-Evidence-based
-Entitlement

Reaction of CDC officials: "Incredulous"
washingtonpost.com/

About 100 million in the northern half of US are under some kind of winter warning, watch or advisory right now

70

Climate Change Chili

Ingredients

1 Can Baked Beans
1 Can Red Beans (drained)
1 Pkg Veggie Crumbles
2 Tbsp Molasses
Paprika
Turmeric

Garlic Powder
Chile Pepper
Cayenne Pepper
Garlic Salt
Shredded Cheese
Fresh Herbs (Oregano or Basil)

Cozy up to Climate Change Chili and enjoy it while you still can

Directions

Mix ingredients together (except for cheese and herbs), heat at medium temperature, approximately 10 Minutes. Top with shredded cheese and fresh oregano or parsley.

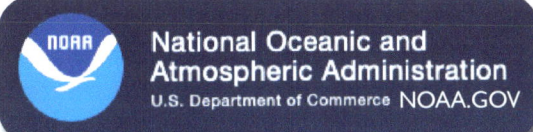
National Oceanic and Atmospheric Administration
U.S. Department of Commerce NOAA.GOV

When the caps melt the ocean currents will shift, causing jet streams to change weather patterns, leading to more extreme natural disasters more often, along with devastating droughts, fires and flooding.

Sierra Club @SierraClub · 12m
They Can't Vote Yet, But Youths Are Ready to #ClimateStrike
sc.org/2LT2BtL via @Sierra_Magazine

They Can't Vote Yet, But Youths Are Ready to #ClimateStrike
We're hurtling toward ecological collapse. Thank goodness your kids are paying attention.
🔗 sierraclub.org

Actor, Business Woman, Activist Jane Fonda, 74, Advocating for Climate Change Action, Arrested at Capital Building, DC 2019

Julie Brethauer
@JulieBrethauer
Replying to @IndivisibleNap @SassyCanadianCk and @MarkTully20

I was absolutely mystified at the MAGA's replies to the announcement that he rolled back vehicle emissions level requirements in California. They were actually cheering the fact that it's ok to put more pollution in the air.

And they call US deranged?!? Unbelievable 🤯

Popular Science @PopSci

New York City isn't ready for the catastrophic floods in its future

Republicans say climate change is a hoax. They are glad Trump doesn't believe in climate change or spends money preparing for it or managing it. Republicans push for less regulation and oversight in mining, coal and oil industries.

Democrats continue to say "WE NEED TO PREVENT OR AT LEAST PREPARE FOR CLIMATE CHANGE NOW!"

Polarized Popularity Pizza

by Common Dreams staff

💬 56 Comments

As *AP* reports, President Donald Trump's "job approval rating sits at just 32 percent, making him the least popular first-year president on record. A quarter of Republicans say they're among those who disapprove of the president." (Image: DonkeyHotey/flickr/cc)

After two years into the Trump Administration, the nation remains deeply divided. As political scandals and disturbing headlines continue to flood the airwaves, the divide grows deeper still. One tweet, in particular illustrates an underlying factor—"The worst part about all of this is realizing how some of your own friends/family are bad people." Family ties and friendships broken over political views are common now and have affected nearly everyone in the nation. But it would be a mistake to label the dividing topic as being merely an opposition over political views. The strong division is drawn from opposing ideals of morals, standards and integrity.   clw

With more than two-thirds of all Americans now disapproving of the job performance of President Donald Trump, a new poll out Saturday shows that he is now the most unpopular U.S. president

"Record Unemployment"

BBC News (World) ✓ · 24m
President Trump wants Americans to start saying "Merry Christmas" ... not "Happy Holidays". What do you say?

 **David Hoffman**
@atDavidHoffman

Here's the thing. I said "Merry Christmas" when Obama was president. So did he. Never felt pressured not to. What's wrong with these freaks?

Replying to @realDonaldTrump
MAGAts are obviously 👌 with racism, tax evasion, extortion, bribery, money laundering, adultery, rape, harassment, lying, cheating but most Americans are not.

Team Trump ✓
@TeamTrump

President @realDonaldTrump has DONE what Nancy Pelosi & the Dems just TALK about!

✅ Lowered prescription drug costs
✅ Negotiated the USMCA
✅ Created the hottest economy in modern history

Thanks, President Trump!

 **Bernie Sanders** ✓
@SenSanders

Republicans are celebrating raising taxes on working families to give tax breaks to billionaires, corporations, private jet owners and themselves. Remember that.

 **Merle Harwood**
@merlin6942

Replying to @FoxNews and @POTUS
Does he know this rhetoric divides the country there are a lot of Democrats out there it shouldn't be about parties it should be country first President should not be talking like this guy does it is not good

6/21/18, 7:49 AM

"BEST PRESIDENT EVER!"
"Better Than Lincoln"

GOP submits shoddy, TAX BILL with hand-written entries overnight, to be voted on next day.

FUN FACT

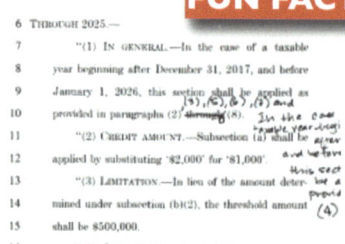

handwriting their tax bill ...
vox.com

 Elizabeth Warren ✓ · 45m
The bill that the Republicans jammed through the Senate tonight isn't tax reform. It's a heist. Let's call this out for what it is: Government for sale.
#GOPTaxScam

💬 257   🔁 2,083   ♡ 4,523

 Elizabeth Warren ✓ · 44m
Americans are angry. And they are right to be angry. Over & over, again & again, they watch this Congress ignore their problems while jumping to do more favors for billionaires, giant

72

Polarized Popularity Pizza

Ingredients

1 Pizza Crust (pre-made)
1/2 C Tbsp Pesto Sauce
1 C Mozzarella Cheese

One Side:
Cherry Tomatoes, halved
Spinach, Onion, Olives chopped

Other half:
Pepperoni and bacon bits

Choose your side and dig in!

Directions

Pre-heat oven to 425° F
Spread the pesto evenly on the pizza crust. Sprinkle the cheese with seasonings to taste. Arrange one half with tomatoes, basil and olives, the other half with pepperoni and bacon bits. Bake for about 10-15 minutes, until the cheese melts and the crust becomes golden brown and crispy..
Choose your side and enjoy!

Joe Walsh
@WalshFreedom

A caller into the radio show tonight: "Look, I voted for Trump, but I'm tired of all this drama. Everyday is another soap opera. So many tweets & fights. It's exhausting. I'm just really tired of it."

I'm hearing more and more of that these days.

Yahoo News
Trump's 'Civil War' threat is 'beyond repugnant,' says GOP Rep. Kinzinger
President Trump sent out a barrage of tweets over the weekend defending

I don't care if it's tiresome to say it: if a Dem president were acting this way, Republicans would be calling for SEAL teams to seize the White House.

The neighbor hung this up. I shot back a response. Kind of tense in the neighborhood this morning. 😔

Alan Resists
@angry__saint

Just think how far we would be, as a human species, if not for the GOP, Religion & NRA

9:19 AM · Jul 7, 2018 · Twitter for iPhone

Republicans don't seem to care about the polls or that the country is divided.   TRUMP IS THEIR MAN!

Democrats find it hard to believe that the approval ratings and polling numbers aren't lower than 32%. They don't understand why Trump supporters continually vote for Republican laws that hurt the middle class. They think that the latest scandal will end his bases' support—it doesn't.

Literary Lettuce Wrap

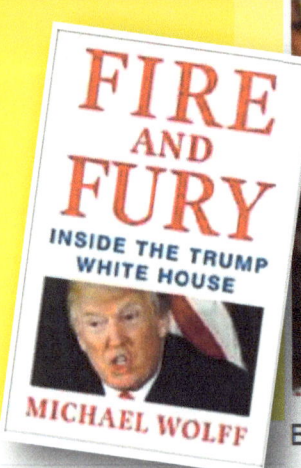

Book on Trump Sells a Million Copies ...
wsj.com

Donald J. Trump
@realDonaldTrump

A low level staffer that I hardly knew named Cliff Sims wrote yet another boring book based on made up stories and fiction. He pretended to be an insider when in fact he was nothing more than a gofer. He signed a non-disclosure agreement. He is a mess!

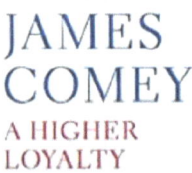

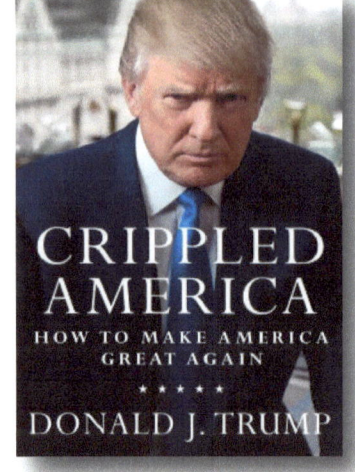

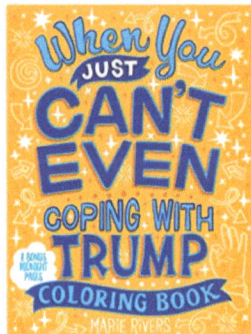

Kids in cages ...

Regardless of your position on the Trump Administration, we can all agree that it has spawned a plethora of literature— fact, fiction and funny.

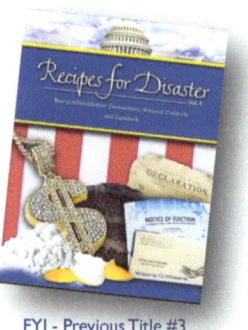

FYI - Previous Title #3

FUN FACT   CBS News

Harry Potter banned: Nashville Catholic school bans "Harry Potter" book series, citing risk of "conjuring evil spirits"

A Catholic school in Nashville, Tennessee has banned the "Harry Potter" series because a reverend at the school claims the books include ...

Literary Lettuce Wrap

Ingredients

- Head of Lettuce (Romain, Butter)
- Cod Fillets
- Olive Oil
- Shredded Carrots
- Cherry Tomatoes
- Pesto

Directions

Literary Lettuce Wrap...It's messy but it's good!

Brush cod with olive oil. Broil the cod until thoroughly cooked. Place on big pieces of lettuce. Add carrots and tomato, top with pesto. For a really great lettuce wrap, march down to that cool bookstore and get yourself a real cookbook.

Many have been inspired to report and/or express their point of view during this highly divided and tumultuous time in American history.

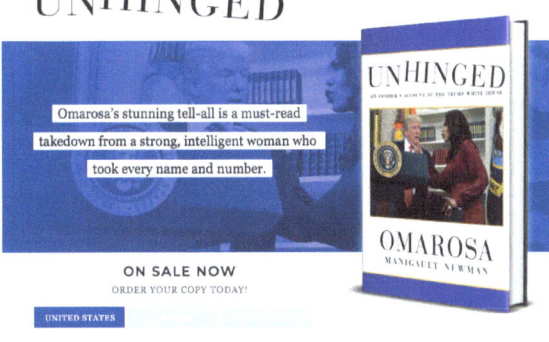

FUN FACT

Republicans don't read. Just kidding!...but there ARE audio books to choose from too...just sayin'...

Democrats have a lot to choose from if they want to 'read-up' on Trump Administration commentary.

Melania Melt

"I really don't care, do U?"

? The Enigma that is Melania ?

Melania Melt

Ingredients

- 1 Can of Tuna
- 2 Tbsp Mayonnaise
- 2 Slices Cheddar Cheese
- 4 Slices of Multigrain Bread
- 2 Tomato Slices
- Oregano
- Crushed Red Pepper
- Olive Oil

Directions

Melania can make your heart melt...or your brain melt depending on you point of view, either way, enjoy this tuna melt!

Mix up the tuna, set aside. Melt an ample amount of coconut oil, olive oil on a hot grill. Place the bread slices on the griddle and spoon tuna one slice. Top with tomato slices if desired. Place cheese slices on other slice and heat for a few minutes on medium heat. Sprinkle with seasonings and place the bread with cheese slice over the bread with the tuna and heat for another minute or so.

Always Best To Cover Your Assets....

 Julia Ioffe @juliaioffe

RNC notes say Melania Trump received degree in design. False. She dropped out after a year, but campaign keeps talking about her degree.

Legal status of Melania Trump's parents raises questions about 'chain migration'

By KATHERINE FAULDERS AND DEVIN DWYER Feb 22, 2018, 12:55 PM ET

Uncle Mike - Wartime Consigliere @MichaelPacholek · Jul 19, 2016
Replying to @juliaioffe
Melania Trump graduated from Princeton, and then from Harvard Law. Oh, wait, no, that was Michelle Obama again.

Republicans are OK with Melania lying about having a degree to gain US citizenship. They are also OK with Melania's questionable background and her parents' criminal record and mob ties, saying, "I REALLY DON'T CARE, DO U?"

Democrats feel Melania's background and questionable citizenship issues should be taken seriously especially when immigrant veterans and students are being rounded up, put in cages and deported without due process.

Free-Press Pepperoli

'Naked Attack on the Free Press': Trump Allies Reportedly Raising $2 Million for Campaign to Discredit Journalists

The First Amendment guarantees freedoms concerning religion, expression, assembly, and the right to petition. It forbids Congress from both promoting one religion over others and also restricting an individual's religious practices. It guarantees freedom of expression by prohibiting Congress from restricting the press or the rights of individuals to speak freely. It also guarantees the right of citizens to assemble peaceably and to petition their government.

Journalists with integrity struggle to gain, report and expose the truth. Dodged questions, vague or misleading answers are commonplace. The Trump Administration has openly and routinely disrespected national journalists, calling them "the enemy of the people." Fascist and corrupt governments have utilized false propaganda to manipulate gullible populations. Controlling media outlets and silencing journalists is the first and main step for conducting a dictatorship. When journalists with integrity are being threatened and silenced, BEWARE.
clw

BBC News Cameraman Is Shoved to the ..

Trump's attacks on media raise threat ...
theguardian.com

Replying to @politico
We understand. Just like Putin & Kim Jung Un. Trump doesn't want reporters, reporting the facts.

Free-Press Pepperoli

Ingredients

1 2lb pkg Spinach Ravioli
1 Pkg of Pepperoni
1 Cup Shredded Cheese
1 20 oz jar Tomato Sauce
1 6 oz jar of tomato paste
6 Garlic Cloves, sliced

2 Tsp Olive Oil
1 Tsp ground Turmeric
1 Tsp Garlic Powder
1 Tsp Agave
1/2 Tsp Italian Seasoning
1 Tsp Cayenne Pepper

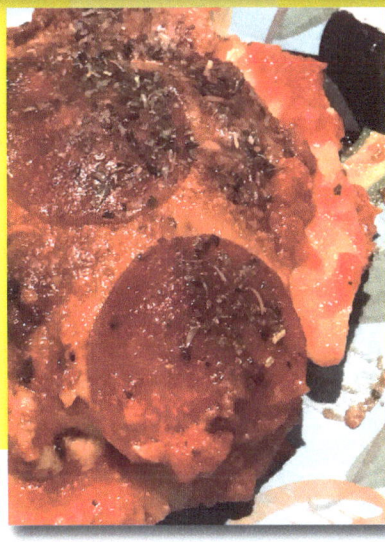

Free-Press Pepperoli - Enjoy a little comfort food while you are fighting for the 1st Amendment

Directions

Ravioli and Pepperoni
Bring 1 quart of water to boil. Place frozen ravioli in boiling water, reduce heat and simmer for 10 minutes. Drain. Set aside. Use medium heat to saute the garlic in the olive oil. Add the tomato paste, the tomato sauce and seasonings. Add the ravioli and mix gently. Transfer the mixture to a 9x9 baking dish and spread evenly. Top with shredded cheese and top the cheese with pepperoni slices to cover. Sprinkle with additional seasoning of your choice. Bake at 375° for 30 minutes.

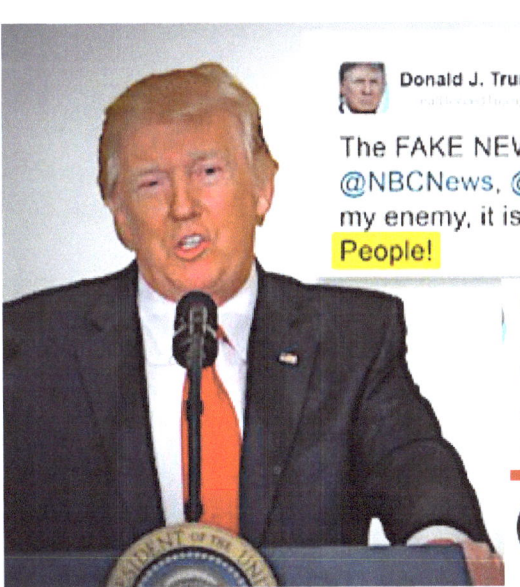

FUN FACT

- Republicans, in particular were targeted for political mis-information tactics aimed at the US 2016 election. Paid Russian, Turkish and other social media experts created 'memes' and false stories designed to cripple the democratic front-runner.
- Democrats were also subjected to dis-information but did not fall for it nearly as much as Republicans and not worth the time and effort, as they did not 'click' and re-circulate bogus memes and articles.

Faith Based Fried Fish

"Thoughts & Prayers"

Evangelical Christians love Trump's racism but call his profanity "blasphemy," and are threatening to stay away from the polls in 2020 because Trump is "using the Lord's name in vain."

...but they are OK with the 'pussy grabbing,' racial hate-voilence and community service funding cuts?

FEED THE HUNGRY
CARE FOR THE SICK
SHELTER THE HOMELESS
LOVE EVERYONE

CUT FOOD STAMP BENEFITS
GUT AFFORDABLE HEALTHCARE
DEMONIZE THE HOMELESS
BLOCK EQUALITY RIGHTS

SO IF THE BIBLE SAYS WE SHOULD HELP THE POOR, WELCOME THE FOREIGNER, HEAL THE SICK, RESPECT OTHERS, NOT LIE, NOT COMMIT ADULTERY, AND NOT STEAL, THEN WHY DO WE SUPPORT DONALD TRUMP?

OH, BILLY. WE DON'T ACTUALLY PRACTICE THESE THINGS. WE ONLY PREACH THEM.

Yet ANOTHER Mass Shooting?!?!?!

"Thoughts & Prayers"

So these "Two Corinthians" walk into a bar...

Christians have been warning about the Antichrist for 2000 years. So when he finally shows up, they vote for him.

Faith Based Fried Fish

Ingredients

Cod (or favorite white fish)
Vegetable Oil
Flour

Bread Crumbs (seasoned)
Garlic Powder

Take faith in this delicious Faith Based Fried fish, it's heavenly!

Directions

Rinse and cut fish into manageable sizes. Combine flour and bread crumbs ingredients (equal parts) in shallow dish or plate. Drag and press fish pieces into flour mixture until thoroughly coated on all sides. Heat oil in frying pan to medium-high heat. Gently drop each piece into hot oil. Turn when bottom side is golden brown. Note: 6 pieces, 6 minutes and 6 seconds. Pray it comes out alright.

Paula White to head Trump's faith office - Religion News Service
https://religionnews.com › 2019/11/01 › paula-white-to-head-trumps-faith-... ▾
Nov 1, 2019 - "Paula White is the Advisor to the (**White House**) Faith & Opportunity Initiative," ... The **appointment** of the popular author and former **pastor** of a ...

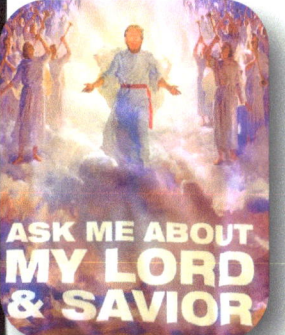

"Thoughts & Prayers"

Quote

Religion is an insult to human dignity. With or without it, you'd have good people doing good things and evil people doing bad things, but for good people to do bad things, it takes religion. - **Steven Weinberg**

Republicans (most) claim to be religious and many believe Trump was chosen by their particular God to 'Make America Great Again,' though we still don't know what time period they are referring to.

Democrats believe in freedom of religion but there should be a **'separation of church and state'** meaning the government should be run **WITHOUT** religious influences that would impede personal freedoms, as stated in the United States Constitution.

Libtard Snowflake Linguine

 lib·tard
/ˈlibˌtärd/

oun INFORMAL • OFFENSIVE

a contemptuous term for a person with left-wing political views.

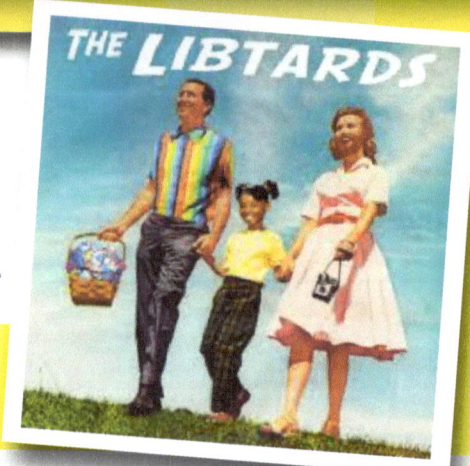

 Amer Khwaja, Born in Wisconsin. Lived in the US my whole life mostly in CA.
Answered Dec 26, 2018 · Author has **13.5k** answers and **2.5m** answer views

Originally Answered: What is meant when people refer to "Libtards"?

It's a contraction of the words 'liberal' and 'retard' (someone of diminished mental capacity) and is meant as an insult to liberals. To me it means they don't have valid arguments and have to instead resort to juvenile name calling to show disagreement with ideas other than their own.

Many "Libtards" are well educated and politically aware.

Liberals (or "Libtards" as some Trump Supporters call them) want the wealthy corporations and the "1%ers" to pay their fair share of taxes instead of using loop-holes and off-shore accounts and getting huge tax-cuts.

They want tax revenue to fund public education, including vocational and higher learner options, as well as community services for everyone in need. "Libtards" also want stricter gun control, equal rights/pay, environmental protection (higher pollution regulations) and green energy technology development and production.

Liberals generally pride themselves on being "PC" (politically correct) meaning, they don't indulge in 'name-calling' or dishonesty and respect others' points of view, e56nough to have a quality conversation.

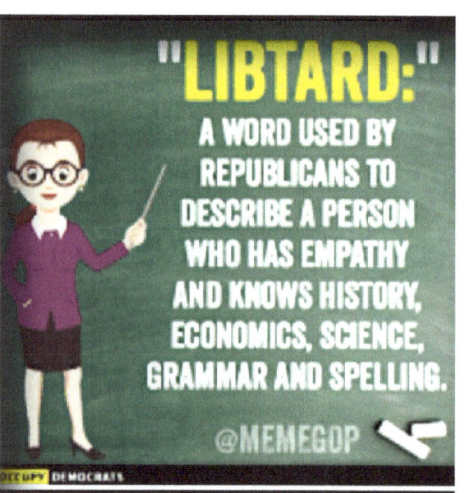

and @TheDemCoalition

Neither did I. I am so sick of being angry or sad every damn day. How do these Republicans just let this go on and on and still sleep at night?

6/22/18, 12:13 PM

 **MusingsofaMisanthrope**
@MusingMsAnthrop

Replying to @PikachuSerena and @dennis0805a

It is nice you tried, but you are right. A conversation without reason, logic or facts is futile at best. I don't even bother to block them – most are 'copy & paste Russian bots anyway.

Some "Libtards" have lost their patience and refuse to correspond with Trump Supporters in any way, citing the 'Chess & Pigeons' metaphor.

Other "Libtards" have started to lash out and abandon their "PC" ways.

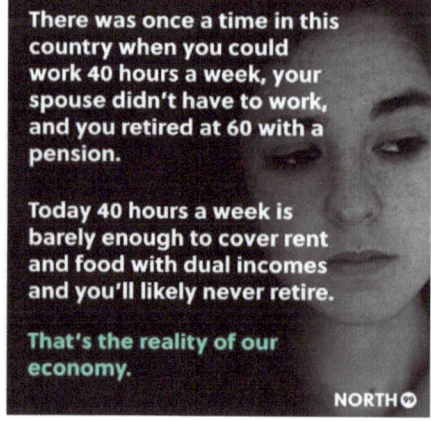

Libtard Snowflake Linguine

Ingredients

1 Pkg Linguine
1 Snow Crab Meat
1 Jar Alfredo Sauce
3 Garlic Cloves
3 Tbsp Olive Oil

*Laugh as you try some Libtard Linguine
They're so funny with all their silly compassionate ways*

Directions

Prepare linguine as directed on package (boil for 15 min until tender and sensitive). Drain and set aside. Saute' garlic cloves in the Olive Oil and then add Alfredo sauce over medium heat. **Gently** add the delicate snowflake, I mean snow crab and continue to heat another 10 minutes.

Some 'Libtards' are finding it very difficult to maintain the "high road" while dealing with Trump Supporters and watching US morals and integrity fall by the way side under Trump. They feel Republicans need to be held accountable.

I pledge allegiance to the RESISTANCE of the United States of America and to the ideals for which it stands one nation, free of hatred with kindness and acceptance for ALL

Chess & Pigeons Metaphor

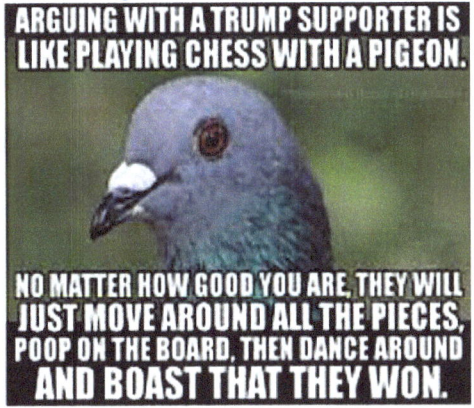

Republicans usually use name-calling in their communications. "Libtard" (Liberal and retarded) is a particular favorite. Trump himself routinely uses derogatory nick-names for his opposition.

Democrats generally tend to refrain from using derogatory nick names in communications. They feel it deteriorates the level of communication and shows a lack of intellect and integrity...though some are straying from that "high road" as tensions persist.

83

Cult 45 Pale Ale

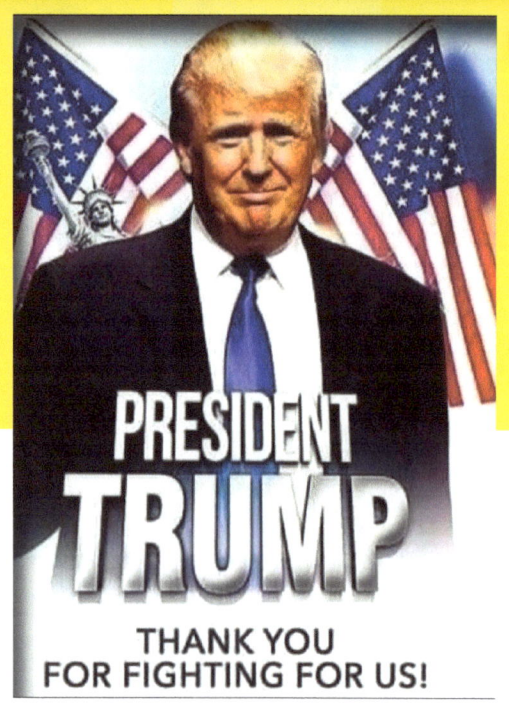

"We're doing God's work"

Meet Trump's right hand man who advocated separating children from their parents at the US-Mexico border
read.bi/2t8eovG

TRUMP
Senior Advisor
White Nationalist, Stephen Miller

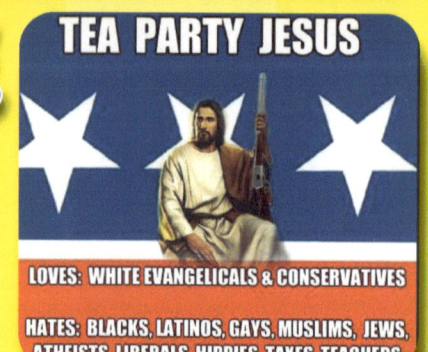

TEA PARTY JESUS

LOVES: WHITE EVANGELICALS & CONSERVATIVES
HATES: BLACKS, LATINOS, GAYS, MUSLIMS, JEWS, ATHEISTS, LIBERALS, HIPPIES, TAXES, TEACHERS

🇺🇸 Super Elite Texan...

QUOTES FROM DONALD TRUMP:

 "I'll beat the crap outta you"

"Part of the problem is... nobody wants to hurt each other anymore..."

"The audience hit back...thats what we need more of..."

 "Knock the crap outta them"

"I'd like to punch him in the face"

"If you do (hurt him) I'll defend you in court. Dont worry"

 "If (Hillary) she gets to pick her judges, theres nothing you can do... although with the 2nd Amendment people, maybe there is..." (Guns)

 BI Business Insider ✓
@businessinsider

Neo-Nazi Marine accused of attacking a protestor at Charlottesville rally found guilty at court-martial — via
@TaskandPurpose

84

Cult 45 Pale Ale

Ingredients

8.5 lbs. 2-Row base malt
1.5 lbs. Crystal Malt
0.5 lbs. CaraPils
0.65 ounces Centennial Hops (11%AA) for 60 minutes
0.5 ounces Centennial Hops (11%AA) for 15 minutes
0.5 ounce Centennial Hops (11%AA) for 1 minute (at flame-out)
1 tsp. Irish Moss or other fining agent (15 minutes)
Yeast Options: Fermentis SafAle US-05, Wyeast 1056, or White Labs WLP001

A Pale Ale seems to be most appropriate for Cult 45

Directions

Mash at 152° F for one hour.
Mash out at 170° F and sparge.
Bring wort to a boil and add 0.65 ounces of Centennial Hops at 11%AA.
After 45 minutes, add 0.5 ounces of Centennial Hops and Irish Moss.
After 15 more minutes, turn off heat,
add 0.5 ounces of Centennial hops, and stir well.
Chill to 68° F and rack to fermenter.
Pitch yeast and ferment at 68 degrees F for 7-10 days or until fermentation is complete.
Bottle or keg and carbonate to 2.5 volumes of carbon dioxide.

Batch Size:	5 gallons
Original Gravity:	1.054
Efficiency:	75%
Final Gravity:	1.012
SRM:	6.6L
IBUs:	43
ABV:	5.5%

Republicans don't care if Trump Administration is under-going several national and state level investigations, including guilty pleas and indictments. They say the investigations are a "Witch Hunt" fabricated by the "Deep State" and even if Trump is found guilty, it wouldn't matter to them. They feel they are discriminated against and he will fight for them.
Democrats will have a Pale Ale and anything else to ease the pain of what they see as being the worst political circus of all time with an unqualified, incompetent and dangerous Administration at the helm.

Go Back Baked Alaska

Go back where you came from - Wikipedia
https://en.wikipedia.org › wiki › Go_back_where_you_came_from ▼
"**Go back** where **you came from**" is a racial insult used in the United States to target immigrants or members of minority groups who are falsely regarded as immigrants. There is also a common variant of this phrase popularized by the Ku Klux Klan "**Go back** to your country."
Background · Examples · Global usage

POLITICS
Trump tells progressive congresswomen to 'go back' to where they came from
PUBLISHED SUN, JUL 14 2019·10:53 AM EDT   UPDATED MON. JUL 15 2019·6:02 AM EDT

By NOLAN D. MCCASKILL
10/04/2019 08:22 PM EDT

At one point, Trump also credited African Americans for building the country, a seeming reference to their ancestors' role as slaves.

"You know, you're just starting to get real credit for that, OK," Trump said. "I don't know if you know that, you're just starting to get — you built the nation. We all built it, but you were such a massive part of it. Bigger than you were given credit for. Does that make sense?"

Donald Trump tells US congresswomen to ...
abc.net.au   "The Squad"

Immigration Documents ...
issc.asu.edu

If you are black, chances are good that your roots in America were planted long before any of the ignorant, racist assailants.

If America was being attacked and living conditions became unbearable, what would you do, where would you go -- and what if they didn't let you in?

'Go back to China': Racist white woman goes berserk after she allegedly hits 'chinky' Asian woman's car

Published 2 months ago on August 25, 2019
By David Edwards

86

Go Back Baked Alaska

Ingredients

2 quarts Vanilla Ice Cream
1 package White Cake Mix
1 Egg, 8 Egg Whites
1/2 tsp Almond Extract
1/8 tsp Cream of Tartar
1/8 tsp Salt
1 C Sugar

Go Back Baked Alaska will make you yearn for your homeland...if you are the of the Caucasian persuasion

Directions

Line the bottom and sides of an 8-inch round mixing bowl or deep 8-inch square container with foil. Spread ice cream in container, packing firmly. Cover and freeze 8 hours or until firm.
Preheat oven to 350 degrees F (175 degrees C). Grease and flour an 8x8 inch pan.
Prepare cake mix with egg and almond extract. Pour into prepared pan.
Bake in preheated oven according to package instructions, until center of cake springs back when lightly touched.
Beat egg whites with cream of tartar, salt and sugar until stiff peaks form.
Line a baking sheet with parchment or heavy brown paper. Place cake in center. Turn molded ice cream out onto cake. Quickly and prettily spread meringue over cake and ice cream, all the way to paper to seal. Return to freezer 2 hours. Preheat oven to 425, Bake the Alaska 8 to 10 minutes, or until meringue is lightly browned. Serve at once.

Go Back To Russia, And Take Your Lying, Cheating, Racist, Hateful Ways With You!

Get information about your rights and how to protect yourself against discrimination and Illegal acts.

KNOW YOUR RIGHTS — American Civil Liberties Union ACLU.org

Everyone has basic rights under the U.S. Constitution and civil rights laws. Learn more here about what your rights are, how to exercise them, and what to do when your rights are violated.

Republicans are known for spouting racist tropes towards Mexicans, Blacks, Asians, Jews and even Native Americans.

Democrats continue to extend compassion for immigrants seeking a better way of life and generally welcome those in need without feeling their own livelihood is being threatened.

K-9 Rump Roast

dog caught mauling handcuffed ...
Lawsuit seeks damages

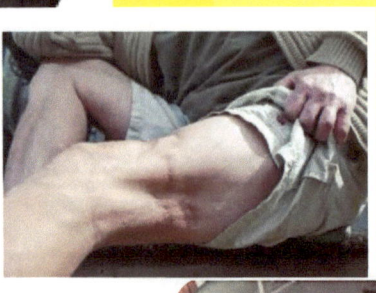

770,000 paid out to police dog bite ...

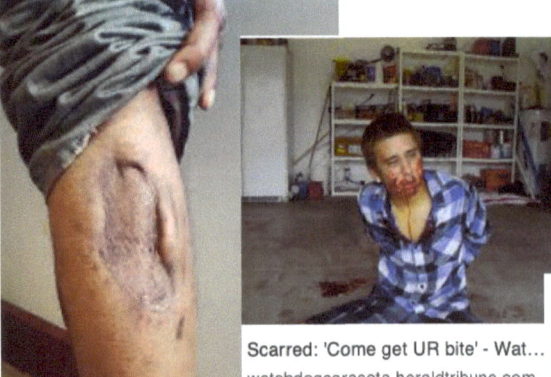
Scarred: 'Come get UR bite' - Wat...
watchdogsarasota.heraldtribune.com
Can Gory Police Dog A...

Police Dog Mauls Innocent 52-Year-Old ...

Dog Chews Arm of Innocent Woman Taking Out the Trash

Attack Dog Bites Reporter ...
youtube.com

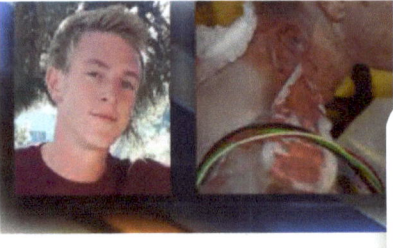
Lawsuit says police ordered K-9 ...
thedenverchannel.com

vestigation into police dog attack ...

What could go wrong there?

NBC4 Washington
Former Navy SEAL Trains Cloned K-9s to Locate and Take Down School Shooters
He began training police dogs to detect drugs or explosives, teaching ... During the demonstration, the dog aggressively attacks Jimmy once he ...
Aug 13, 2019

WPEC
Riviera Beach police officer disciplined after K-9 attack caught ...
It ended with the police dog repeatedly biting the suspect. Officials determined the officer violated department policy and disciplined him.
Apr 9, 2019

KGO-TV
New Mexico Police K-9 attacks unarmed man during welfare check, officer under investigation
CLOVIS, N.M. -- Three police officers and the department are facing a lawsuit after a man said the officers allowed a police dog to attack him in ...
May 24, 2019

FUN FACT

The use of K-9 Units has been abused. The Officers' job is to restrain/arrest and bring in for 'due process,' not injure or kill.

Horrifying moment as police dog attacks innocent bystander ...
https://www.dailymail.co.uk › news › article-7498745 › Police-dog-gets-a... ▾
Sep 24, 2019 - Horrifying footage has captured a **police K9 attacking** an innocent bystander in Vancouver, Washington. ... It took the officers to loosen the **dog's** grip from the man's arm. ... He added that the **police dog** did not appear to be following the cop's commands. ... The Vancouver **Police** Department is ...

K-9 Rump Roast

Ingredients

Beef Roast
1/4 C Olive Oil

1/4 C Worcester Sauce
Cracked Pepper & Salt

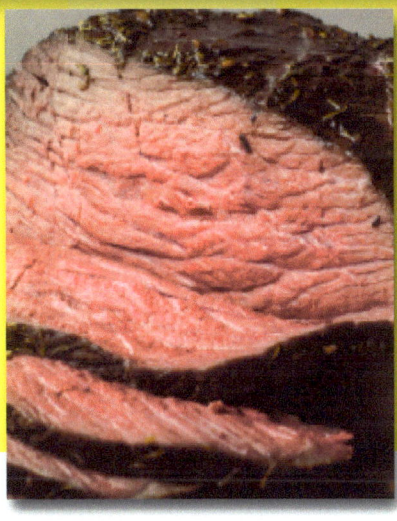

Take a big bite out of this rump, so satisfying and juicy!

Directions

Rinse meat and place in lightly oiled roasting pan or baking dish. Combine Olive Oil and Worcester Sauce and seasoning in a small dish. Poke holes in roast with a fork, then brush or spoon mixture over roast. Roast at 325° for 1 1/2 - 2 hours until the roast reaches 135°F for medium rare or 145°F for medium well.

Police Dog attacks are violent and vicious. They mutilate suspects, sometimes fatally

 CBC.ca

Child seriously hurt after being attacked by father's police dog in training

A child was seriously injured after he was bitten by his father's police dog

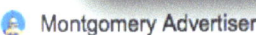 Montgomery Advertiser

Family of Montgomery man killed by police dog sues city

Joseph Pettaway died on July 8 after a police dog attacked him inside a Montgomery home. He died of a ruptured artery in his thigh, according ...
Jan 4, 2019

 Phoenix New Times

Man Seeks $2M After Arizona Police Dog Chewed Half His ...

Video: Arizona Police Dog Chewed Half Man's Face Off. He's Seeking $2 ... After the dog releases the bite, the officer wearing the body camera ...
Jul 12, 2019

Republicans praise Law Enforcement along with their K-9 Units.

Democrats still condemn Law Enforcement excessive force, including the K-9 Units.

Blissful Beef Burgundy

What Climate Change? What Discrimination? What Poverty? What Police Brutality? What Border Security Issue? What Gun Violence? What Drug Addiction Epidemic? What Pollution? What Healthcare Problems? What Skyrocketing Deficit?

'Ignorance is Bliss' as the saying goes, but that saying doesn't tell of the reaction when the troubles come to your own front door. Some people, (even though they did not vote for Trump and don't like his policies) feel that their particular life is not impacted, therefore they see no need to worry about anything. Conversely, some people, have the ability to foresee the repercussions of reduced EPA & CDC standards, reduced banking regulations, ban on abortions, police brutality, pay discrimination and fracking/mining run-off.

History has shown us that reduced EPA standards have resulted in numerous cases of detrimental water poisoning. History also reveled an increase in crime and poverty due partly to anti-abortion laws..* Unbridled police brutality has lead to deaths of innocent people and destructive retaliation riots. Reduced banking regulations can lead to another national recession. We have seen all of this to be true but some people have no access to such information, while others actually choose to be ignorant.   clw   *Freakonomics by Dubner/Levitt

RadicalMooseLamb
@FireZMissiles

Replying to @FoxNews and @POTUS

When a crowd of people are still chanting "lock her up" a year and a half after the election, not even a week after his campaign manager went to jail - we've got a serious problem.

6/21/18, 7:43 AM

RELATIONSHIPS NEVER DIE A NATURAL DEATH. THEY ARE ALWAYS MURDERED BY ATTITUDE, BEHAVIOR, EGO, OR IGNORANCE.

THERE IS NO GREATER POVERTY THAN IGNORANCE

Tucker Carlson: Keeping Immigrant Families Together Threatens 'Your Country'

"No matter what they tell you, this is not about helping children," the Fox News host said.

By Michelle Lou

Fox News host Tucker Carlson has vilified critics of the Trump administration's strict family separation policy, framing the

Blissful Beef Burgundy

Ingredients

2 lb top round Steak, cubed
1 large Onion, sliced
1 clove Garlic, minced
1/3 C Flour
1 can (10 oz) Beef Broth,
1/2 cup Red Wine

1/2 tsp Thyme
8 oz fresh Mushrooms, sliced
1/4 tsp Black Pepper
1 pkg Egg Noodles, cooked

Experience bliss when you try this Blissful Beef Burgundy. It's hard not to acknowledge!,

Directions

Heat a large skillet over medium high heat. Add steak and saute until browned, about 5 minutes. Place in a slow cooker. Put sliced onion and garlic in same skillet and coat with cooking spray. Saute for 5 minutes or until the onions are translucent. Sprinkle flour over the top and cook for another minute, stirring occasionally. Add broth, wine, and tomato paste, stirring constantly. Cook for about 1 minute or until thickened. Add whole onions, thyme, mushrooms, salt, pepper, and bay leaf. Pour into the slow cooker over the beef. Cover and cook on High for 1 hour. Reduce to Low and cook an additional 4 1/2 hours. Discard bay leaf and serve over egg noodles.

Republicans do not doubt Trump's words or FOX News and believe all other news outlets are "Fake News" like Trump says. They really don't care to hear anything different.

Democrats seem to be more savvy at recognizing truly "fake news" and usually view several different news sources. Checking the source has become standard procedure for many.

Wait. What? Halibut

ACLU ✓
@ACLU

The Trump administration is saying that it can secretly lock up a U.S. citizen and bar us from trying to help him.

The Trump Administration Just Admitted a Secretly Detained Americ...

The Washington Post

BIG MACS, SCREAMING FITS AND CONSTANT RIVALRIES

Scenes from the Trump campaign

BY MICHAEL KRANISH
DECEMBER 2 AT 7:05 PM

Elton John blares so loudly on Donald Trump's campaign plane that staffers can't hear

NOVEMBER 28 34°

TOP STORIES

CNN
North Korea: New missile test shows all of US in range

Paul Ryan Struggles To Explain Why Trump Shouldn't Have To Resign Over Sexual Misconduct Claims

He said he's only focused on misconduct in Congress.

By Willa Frej

NPR ✓
@NPR

FUN FACT

The NRA may have accepted more contributions from Russian donors than it first acknowledged, new documents show.

US homeless people numbers rise for first time in seven years

🕐 06 December 2017   US & Canada

Ian Pannell reports from the city of Baltimore: "Hope has given way to despair"

The number of homeless people in the United States has increased for the first time since 2010.

A group of American senators will travel to #Russia at the end of the month and celebrate Independence Day in Moscow. ⚠️ American. Senators. Will. Celebrate. Independence. Day. In. Russia. ⚠️

American senators to visit Russia at end of month: repor...
nydailynews.com

NBC NEWS
A Panama tower carries Trump's name and ties to organized crime

TECHNOLOGY

FUN FACT

engadget
Pentagon left public intelligence gathering data on exposed server

92

Wait. What? Halibut

Ingredients

Fresh Halibut Fillet
3 Tsp Olive Oil
1 Tsp Hemp Seed Oil
1/4 tsp Sage (ground)
1/4 tsp Oregano
1/4 tsp Ginger (ground)
1/4 tsp Green Tea Powder

Be surprised at all the things you didn't know were going on, while you enjoy some Wait What Halibut

Directions

Rinse fillet and place on lightly oiled baking dish. Set aside. Combine Olive oil and Hemp seed oil in a small dish. Add sage, Oregano, Ginger and Green Tea powder. Mix well and pour over fillet. Bake at 400° for approximately 15-20 minutes.

Politico — Trump praises Saudi crown prince, ignores questions on Khashoggi killing
Earlier, before their breakfast at the Imperial Hotel in Osaka, Trump and Prince Mohammed ignored at least two questions about Khashoggi's...
Jun 29, 2019

politics — Donald Trump's Twitter feed is getting more and more bizarre
Analysis by Chris Cillizza, CNN Editor-at-large
2:25 PM EDT June 18, 2018

U.S. HuffPost — Navy Confirms: Those UFO Videos Are Real And Never Should've Been Released
US Navy confirms multiple UFO videos are real **FUN FACT**

The Hill @thehill — JUST IN: Trump VA slashes funding for program that helps homeless veterans obtain housing: report hill.cm/VK8PAoK

The US is now the only country in the world to reject the Paris climate deal
Syria joined the deal today
By Alessandra Potenza | November 7, 2017 10:27 am

Republicans are still spending time, $$ and resources investigating HRC even though she has testified several times and has been cleared of allegations.

FUN FACT
State Dept. intensifies email probe of Hillary Clinton's former aides
washingtonpost.com
5:06 PM · 9/28/19 · Twitter Web Client

Republicans have brought back the coal industry, lessened pollution regulations and diverted tax payer money from FEMA and the military to build the wall. US backed out of the Paris Accord and congratulate Putin on Russian re-elections, while opponents and journalists are threatened and missing. More "Winning."

Democrats are often shocked and dismayed at the rapid deterioration of social standards and corrupt happenings around the world.

Mid-Term Mozzarella

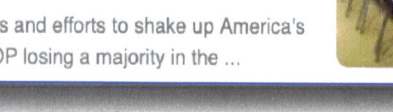

Democrats' blue wave was much larger than early takes suggested

With all votes counted, it's a larger landslide than 1994 or 2010.

By Matthew Yglesias | @mattyglesias | matt@vox.com | Nov 13, 2018, 8:00am EST

By Matthew Yglesias, VOX
The narrative that congealed election night before polls had even closed on the West Coast was that while Democrats may have taken the House, they also underperformed relative to expectations and the hoped-for blue wave had turned into, in the words of columnist Nick Kristof at the New York Times, "only a blue trickle."

This was a questionable interpretation at the time it was offered, but subsequent events have shown it to be almost entirely a psychological illusion based on timing.

Like in any election, Democrats both won some squeakers and lost some squeakers. They overperformed expectations in some races and underperformed them in others. And in 2018, it happens to be the case that Democrats got some of their most disappointing results in East Coast states with early closing times, while the GOP's biggest disappointments came disproportionately in late-counting states.

Consequently, what felt to many like a disappointment as of 11 pm Eastern time on election night now looks more and more like a triumph.

Trump holds last-ditch flurry of rallies ahead of midterm elections

President is embarking on frenzied dash across the US with nine rallies in eight states in effort to hang onto Republican control

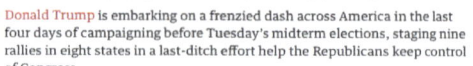

Donald Trump is embarking on a frenzied dash across America in the last four days of campaigning before Tuesday's midterm elections, staging nine rallies in eight states in a last-ditch effort help the Republicans keep control of Congress.

Replying to @thehill
Wait! What happened to the **Blue Wave**, @NateSilver538? I thought A Dem Storm was coming?

U.S. News & World Report
Report: Trade, Health Care Cost GOP Seats in 2018 Midterms
President Donald Trump's tit-for-tat tariffs and efforts to shake up America's trade relationships contributed to the GOP losing a majority in the …

ABC News Politics @ABCPolitics · Sep 10
BREAKING: 38% of Americans approve of Pres. Trump, down from a career-high 44% in July, new @ABC News/Washington Post poll finds; 56% disapprove. abcn.ws/34zjzps

Mid-Term Mozzarella

Ingredients

Fresh Basil
Fresh Tomato
Fresh Cucumber
Fresh Mozzarella Balls

Candie Pecans
Balsamic Glaze
Salt & Pepper

Mid-Term Mozzarella can be a little messy but well worth the effort.

Directions

Thinly slice the mozzarella, tomato and cucumber. Chop the basil. Layer the ingredients; cucumber on the bottom, mozzarella, tomato, then basil on top. Drizzle with Balsamic dressing, salt and pepper to taste.

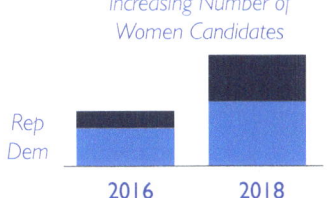

Increasing Number of Women Candidates

Rep
Dem
2016   2018

medit8now @medit8now · 45m
Replying to @Lezdo69 and @Delavegalaw
We voted in a massive **blue wave** in **midterms**. We voted for accountability. Lack of accountability is a cause for apathy.

An unusual Presidency is matched with an unusual 2018 Mid-Term Election

Highest Voter Turnout in Decades

The time and money spent on the numerous Trump Rallies in support of Republican politicians is unprecedented.

The number of women candidates doubled and a few states changed color.

Replying to @bigsurdanapoint @RachelBitecofer and 4 others
The 2018 **blue wave** was not driven by moderate/centrist voters. It was driven by turnout of new voters and voters who didn't usually come out in **midterms**.

SmartDissent.com @smartdissent · Sep 10
We #ResistTrump to save our country. We showed our strength with #BlueWave2018. We must continue with the same energy every day until the 2020 election so we can make progress & improve lives of millions.
#SmartDissent #TheResistance #WeThePeople #StayWoke
smartdissent.com

Republicans ramp up for Mid-Term elections as Trump endorses Roy Moore (known pedophile) and other GOP politicians. Trump energizes rallies across the nation with his 'off-script' style, boasting about the great economy and low unemployment rate.

Democrats continue with protests and voter awareness programs. They managed to 'flip the House,' and turned some long standing Red ground to Blue, though the overall feeling at the time was anti-climatic at best.

Tariff Tortilla

American tariffs are having a bigger impact on US-based Amazon vendors than their...

TechCrunch

MSNBC ✓ @MSNBC · 7h
Bob Kuylen, vice president of the North Dakota Farmer's Union, says he lost $400,000 because of Pres. Trump's trade war with China. He says farmers have "pretty much lost all of our markets since Trump took over."

Farmers rips Trump trade: we've lost everything since...

THE WALL STREET JOURNAL.
Trump Says Companies, Not Trade Policies, to Blame for Business Setbacks

 Vox

Trump's trade war with China is hurting farmers, but they won't abandon him — yet

Beto O'Rourke said he would remove all tariffs on China on his first day in ... "Pretty much out in farm country, we're all Trump supporters," Daryl ...

The New York Times
Trump Says He Will Raise Existing Tariffs on Chinese Goods to 30%
Mr. Trump's stiff tariffs on Chinese goods have been met with .... derail the negotiations and could unsettle supporters during an election year.
3 weeks ago

Trump as 'Tariff Man' Is Still a Hit With Republicans
https://morningconsult.com › 2019/05/22 › trump-as-tariff-man-is-still-a-h... ▼
May 22, 2019 - A Morning Consult/Politico poll found 84 percent of Republican **voters** said they have confidence in **Trump's** ability to negotiate a better trade ...

 CNBC
'It's not a free market': These manufacturers say tariffs help level the playing field with China
Some U.S. manufacturers say tariffs, if targeted, will help address longstanding unfair trade practices like intellectual property theft.

NowThis ✓ @nowthisn... · 1h
This farmer, hit hard by the China trade war, believes Trump is 'backstabbing' the people who got him into office

Maine lobster exports plunge 84% since 2018 tariffs ...
https://www.newscentermaine.com › article › news › maine-lobsters-plung
May 14, 2019 - PORTLAND, **Maine** — It's been 11 m[onths since] **tariffs** were announced and the **Maine** International

FUN FACT

Maine lobster takes tariff hit, Canada picks up slack | National ...
https://www.nationalfisherman.com › News & Views › Northeast ▼
Aug 29, 2019 - **Maine lobster** takes **tariff** hit, Canada picks up slack. The escalating U.S.-China trade war is taking its toll on U.S. **lobster** exports. Growing middle-class demand for live U.S. **lobster** in China boosted U.S. exports in the years before China imposed a 25 percent **tariff** in July 2018.

Tariff Tortilla

Ingredients

- Tortilla
- Shredded Cheese
- Garlic Powder
- Sage
- Oregano
- Italian Seasoning
- Fresh Spinach
- Tomato, Thin Sliced

Tariff Tortilla,...some like it, some don't

Directions

Place tortilla on a well oiled pan with medium heat. Sprinkle shredded cheese to cover tortilla. Sprinkle seasonings onto of the cheese and then place spinach and tomato slices on one half of the tortilla. Fold in half. Heat for another minute or so. Enjoy!

Tariff Definition - What is Tariff - Shopify
https://www.shopify.com › encyclopedia › tariff

A **tariff** is a tax imposed by a government on goods and services imported from other countries that serves to increase the price and make imports less desirable, or at least less competitive, versus domestic goods and services.

The Cost of the Trade War

Tariffs are taxes that Americans pay. These taxes are being paid by American farmers, retailers, manufacturers, businesses and consumers.

Business HuffPost
Fed-Up Farmer's Message To Trump: I Wouldn't Vote For You If You Walked On Water
Chris Gibbs, a former Republican county chair in Ohio, says he's done with Donald Trump.

Trump claims a victory in China trade war, but US farmers want details
AFP

Farmers Turn Backs On Trump
HuffPost

Donald Trump punishes supporters ...
chippewa.com

Republicans are divided on 'Trump's Trade War.' Although some businesses are feeling the impact and some are losing their farm, they believe it will pay-off in the long run.

Democrats generally don't share the same faith in Trump or his policies, that Republicans have.

Rotten Tomatoes

"Most Americans Won't or Can't Do Farm Work"

Some farmers have tried to hire American workers. "Locals," (non-mexican) 3 or 4 out of 50 were worth anything... far as being a good worker"

"They Ain't Durable Enough"

"After 2 or 3 hours, they say, "I can't take it. I gotta quit."

Farmers Can't Find Enough Workers to Harvest Crops—and ...
www.eatingwell.com › ... › Green and Sustainable Eating ▾
Rotten, blackened **fruits** lay among invading weeds on the loamy soil. ... The shortage of labor had forced him to perform **farming's** version of triage and abandon ...

US farmers, desperate for help, increasingly turn to Mexico ...
https://www.csmonitor.com › USA › Politics › US-farmers-desperate-for-hel...
Jun 22, 2018 - But many **farmers** in Trump country find they have no choice; no one ... shortage of pickers forced them to leave some crops **rotting** in the field.

Rotten Tomatoes

Ingredients

- 1 Pkg Lentils (pre-cooked)
- 1 Can Red Beans
- 6 Grape Tomatoes
- Fresh Shredded Parmesan
- 2 Tbsp Hemp Seeds
- Cayenne Pepper
- Salt

Eat up! You're gonna need your strength!

Directions

Heat lentils and red beans in a sauce pan on medium heat until nice and hot (10 min). Top with cheese tomatoes and fresh herbs.

Farmers who align with stricter immigration laws and enforcement (ICE) are left with rotting fruit and vegetables.

~~~~~

"They (white workers) just won't and/or can't do more than a few hours, then they quit. We can't get reliable help no more."

FUN FACT Immigrants work extraordinarily hard for long hours with very little pay. The fear of increased ICE raids reduced the farm labor force by at least 50%

US can grow its own farm workers …

Republican farmers are divided on the stricter immigration laws but all will agree—Ya just can't get good help these days…

Democrats want an immigration policy that makes sense. They believe there can be a healthy balance between immigrant workers and policy.

Farmer French Toast

Farmers Have Mixed Feelings

While some farmers will remain loyal to Trump, regardless of outcome, others are starting to doubt their allegiance to the administration.

Farmers' Frustration With Trump Grows as U.S. Escalates China …
https://www.nytimes.com › 2019/08/27 › politics › trump-farmers-china-trade
1 day ago - WASHINGTON — Peppered with complaints from **farmers** fed up with President **Trump's** trade war, Sonny Perdue found his patience wearing …

 Farmers for Trump shared a post.
March 15 ·

Some of the better lines from this week's Growing America Story:
"You need to ask an older farmer."
"Bad years and good years, that's farming."
"My wife makes me go to church now."
"During a bad year, you need a good woman."

US Tariffs Have Driven Buyers to Other Countries For Produce and Goods.

U.S. has paid more than $1M in interest for late bailout payments to farmers

NBC News **FUN FACT**

 **Farmers for Trump**
January 8, 2018 ·
President Trump spending some time with farmers today... What would you like to share with the President if you had the opportunity?

POLITICO.COM
Trump, in speech to farmers, aims to shore up rural support
The president will tout deregulatory efforts but likely avoid commitment...

 **Farmers for Trump**
August 25 at 9:46 AM ·

This is a plus for our farmers! China choose NOT to to make a deal to buy USA corn from our farmers. President Trump made a deal with Japan and they accepted! Thank you Japan and President Trump! 🎉
🌽 #ThankAFarmer #ThankyouJapan #ThankyouPresidentTrump #USACorn

 **Farmers for Trump** shared a post.
January 4, 2018 ·

483,263 Views
Fox News was live — in France.
August 25 at 3:33 AM ·

Jeremy McCartney
January 2, 2018 · Tallahassee, FL ·   **WHAT?!?!**

Run To The Farm
November 11, 2016 ·
Great info!!!! So happy to see that two days later he is already working on this! His plan is putting Farming at the very top! Just as important as fuel and ene…
See More

AGVIEW.NET
Trump Campaign announces agricultural advisory committee

100

Farmer French Toast

Ingredients

Bread, 4 slices (multi-grain)
3-4 Eggs

Nutmeg, Cinnamon, Cloves
Buttery Maple Syrup

Rise and shine with some Farmer French Toast, it's gonna be a long day ahead...

Thanks Pat ;)

Directions

Scrabble eggs (use 1 egg per slice, generally). Mix in spices and drag each piece of toast through egg mixture, both sides. Let excess egg mixture drip off. Place coated slices one at a time on greased griddle. Flip each slice after one minute or so and repeat flipping as necessary.
Drizzle with buttery maple syrup.

Iowa corn farmers to Trump: The government put us in 'one hell o...
https://thehill.com › homenews › administration › 459022-iowa-corn-farm... ▼
21 hours ago - "It's time for President **Trump** to make rural America and the [Renewable Fuel Standard] great again. He made promises to American **farmers** ...

Farmers' Frustration With Trump Grows as U.S. Escalates China Fight

The New York Times

1 day ago

Trump's trade war with Canada and Mexico has cost Nebraska farmers more than **$1 BILLION** because of the retaliatory tariffs placed on their products. Nebraska voted for Trump over Clinton by **25%** in 2016 and **THIS** is how he rewards them. **Will Trumpers EVER wake up?**

OCCUPY DEMOCRATS

Republican politicians urge farmers to "take the pain" during Trump's tariff wars. Farmers who still support Trump feel they are being patriotic and will reap the benefits at a later date.

Democrats don't support Trump's tariff war and don't like having to hand out billions of $$ for failing farms because of it. They also note the hypocrisy of farmers accepting socialistic hand-outs.

Stock Market Martini

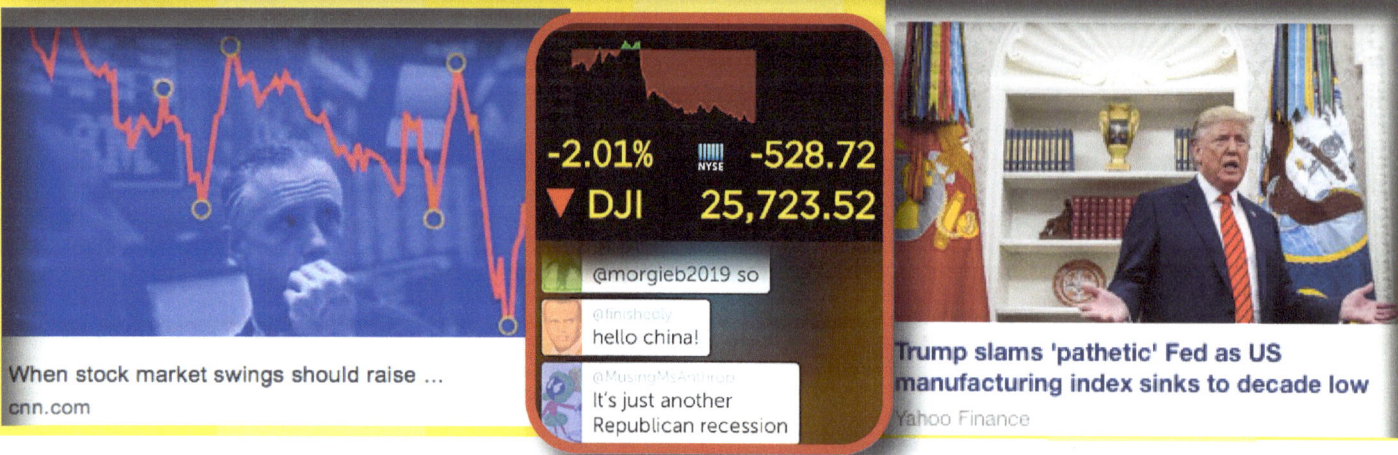

When stock market swings should raise ...
cnn.com

@morgieb2019 so
hello china!
It's just another Republican recession

Trump slams 'pathetic' Fed as US manufacturing index sinks to decade low
Yahoo Finance

"Stock Market Closes At Record High"

Politics Yahoo News
Trump declares himself unimpeachable, based on 'perhaps the greatest economy' ever
"How do you impeach a President who has helped create perhaps the greatest economy in the history of our Country?" Trump asked on Twitter.

F Forbes
Consumers Are At Tipping Point, So Prepare For Bear Stock Market And Recession
It is terrible news. The consumer sentiment results from the University of Michigan Surveys of Consumers have crashed. And the worst part is ...
2 days ago

"The Stock Market Drops, Wiping Out The Previous Gains"

F Forbes
How The Dow's 800-Point Plummet Could Dramatically Hurt The Job Market
Stock market drops, accompanied by the negative sentiment among people and the media fanning the flames of possible recession and even

CNN
Dow jumps nearly 310 points to cap off a crazy week
US stocks rose after bond yields edged up and Europe and China announced plans for additional stimulus to shore up their economies in

 MarketWatch
U.S. stock futures weaken as tariffs go into effect
U.S. stock futures weakened on a holiday Monday as tariffs on Chinese goods went into effect.

"Stock Market Rallies After Plunge"

Stock Market Martini

Ingredients

- Bailys Cherry Chocolate
- Vodka
- Coffee Brandy
- Crushed Ice
- Mint Sprig

Nothing like a decadent Stock Market Martini —Go ahead, splurge a little!

Directions

Pour it in all in a fancy glass and enjoy the great economy while you can.

A **bull market** is a **market** that is on the rise and is economically sound, while a **bear market** is a **market** that is receding, where most stocks are declining in value. Although some investors are "bearish," the majority of investors are "bullish."

"Your 401Ks Will Thank Me!"

 Analyst will always cite multple reasons why a market may crash AFTER it crashes.

Republicans are thrilled that 401Ks are doing great even though many don't have or know what a 401K is. They believe economy is doing better than it ever has, regardless of a skyrocketing deficit, poverty levels and lack of affordable healthcare. They feel they are "Winning!"

Democrats believe the hefty tax breaks for the wealthy and loop-holes for large corporations are contributing to a top-heavy, unbalanced economy and the worst is yet to come, while the 'rich get richer.'

Economical Flatbread

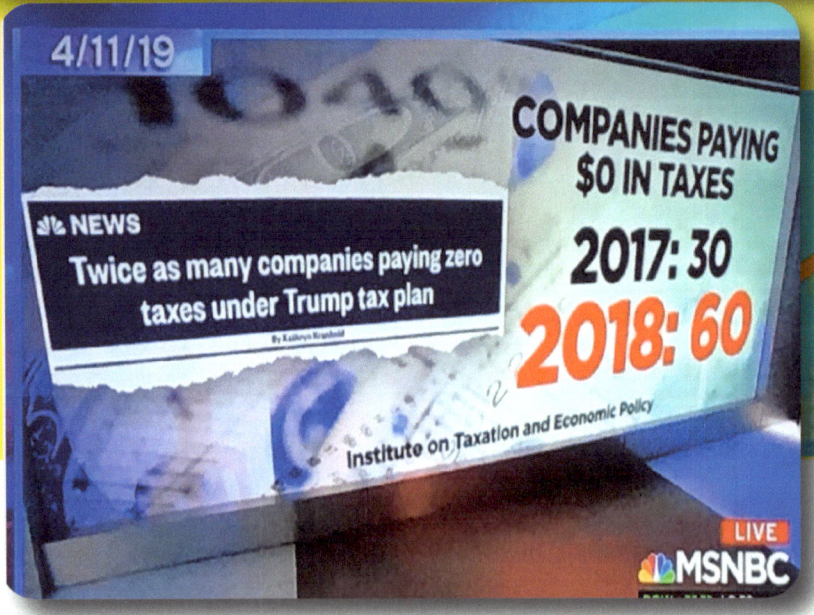

Stock Market Closes at Record High While 'Living Wage' Falls Short

Editorial Board
The World Economy Is Stumbling Toward Disaster

If a new recession strikes, the Trump administration will get – and deserve – much of the blame.

By Editorial Board
October 21, 2019, 3:30 AM MDT

The Stock Market is Breaking Records while poverty levels, living wage, healthcare, education & affordable housing suffer.

The stock market just hit a record high ...

pbs.org

FUN FACT

Amazon, a MULTI-BILLION dollar company pays $0 in taxes

Beware of the 'toxic concoction' that could finally crush the U.S. economy

MarketWatch

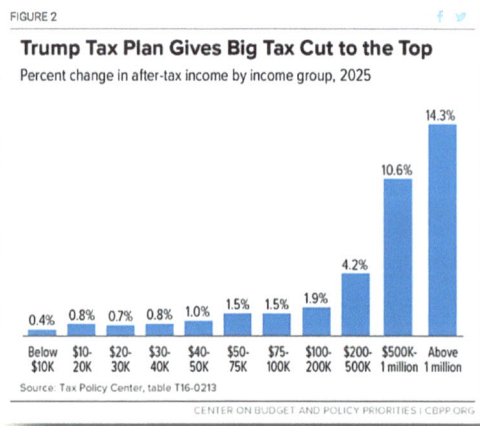

Hiring Steady As Employers Add 136,000 Jobs; Unemployment Dips To 3.5%

October 4, 2019 • U.S. employers added 136,000 jobs in September — a sign of continued resilience in the labor market amid growing signals that the economy is losing steam. The jobless rate was the lowest since 1969.

The New York Times

In a Strong Economy, Why Are So Many Workers on Strike?

At first glance, it may seem like a paradox: Even as the economy rides a 10-year winning streak, tens of thousands of workers across the ...

4 days ago

Caterpillar just flashed the latest warning sign for the global economy

Markets Insider - Busine...

Economical Flatbread

Ingredients

- Flat Bread
- Olive or Coconut Oil
- Fresh Spinach
- Shredded Cheese
- Garlic Cloves
- Mushrooms
- Artichoke
- Feta Crumbles

Directions

Sure the economy is doing great...even though these ingredients seemed pretty expensive!

Dice veggies, set aside. Coat flat bread with oil lavishly. Pile everything on top and bake for 10-15 min. at 375° on top rack.

Worker and Teacher Strikes more prevalent than ever in the US but stocks are yielding returns.

Joe Biden blasts Trump for 'squandering' a strong economy and forgetting the middle...
CNBC.com

Porter 'Does the Math' on the lack of a 'Living Wage.'

FUN FACT

'It's Time To Get Something Back:' Union Workers' Voices Are Getting Louder
Unions and their supporters around the country are assessing whether the United Auto Workers strike against General Motors is a sign of renewed labor power.

Republicans point out the "Great Economy!" and record low unemployment rates.

Democrats don't think the economy is doing all that great, if it takes at least two people to afford an apartment and still have to struggle with groceries and bills.

105

Dystopian Daiquiri

As world's scientists raise extinction alarms, Trump guts Endangered Species Act

BY NOAH GREENWALD, OPINION CONTRIBUTOR — 05/08/19 05:00 PM EDT · 334 COMMENTS

Record Number of Mass Shootings, Natural Disasters & Opioid Overdoses

Oil Spills in North Dakota: What does ...
fractracker.org

Photos of Donald Trump's ...
nydailynews.com

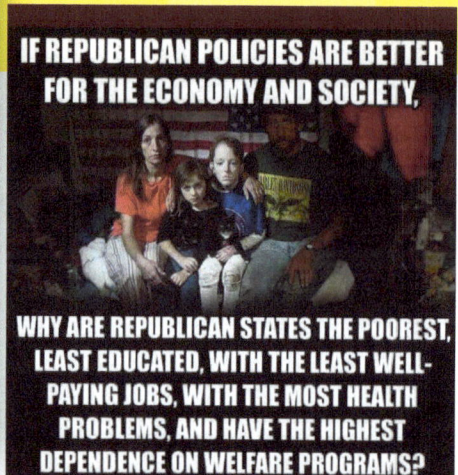

Voter Security Bill Blocked by GOP

Astronomical Healthcare Costs

Trump rolls back decades of Clean Water Act protections - BBC ...
https://www.bbc.com › news › world-us-canada-46526776
Dec 11, 2018 - Trump rolls back decades of **Clean Water Act** protections ... **Trump's** environmental **rollback** rolls on · '**Trump effect**' limits action on climate · The ...

Fiona Adorno @FionaAdorno · 9h
Nazis in the streets, climate-denying fascists in power, national broadcaster publishing propaganda, refugees in cages, earth is dying, Australia's on fire, and now the plague is back. That's right, the Black Death.

FUN FACT

The Washington Post

CDC gets list of forbidden words: Fetus, transgender, diversity

Somebody Is Going to Die": Lawyer ...
democracynow.org

106

Dystopian Daiquiri

Ingredients

Coconut water
Rum
Peppermint drops

Peppermint Sprig
Ice Cubes

Directions

This Dystopian Daiquiri may not be for everyone but it sure does help to ease the pain.

Measure out the needed dosage of rum, pour over ice, add the coconut water, peppermint drops and mint sprig. Good luck with every thing!

Eric and Donald Trump, Jr. own a massive private hunting preserve in upstate New York — and neighbors say it sounds like a 'war zone'

Trump sides with Russia against FBI at ...
bbc.com

While some are worried about the environment, others worry about keeping coal mines open. Some worry about healthcare for all, while others worry about cutting funding for Medicare but they all worry about the stock market and cyber security.

Republicans are not bothered by the numerous accusations of lying, involvement with Russia, inhumanities at detention centers, environmental protection regulation roll-backs, tax evasion and tax breaks for the wealthy while the poverty population increases.

Democrats feel they must be in an alternate/upside-down world where nothing makes sense and is the opposite of what it should be.

People Product Pate

Who's to blame for the nation's opioid crisis? Massive trial may answer that question

Elizabeth Warren · 23h
Nobody having a heart attack or stroke picks their ambulance or ER doc. But when a hospital outsources its physician staffing or ambulance services to a private-equity-owned company, patients can get stuck with outrageous medical bills. It's obscene.

HEALTH + BEHAVIOR

Long-term care hospitals keep patients longer than necessary for financial reasons
David Olmos, UCLA Health

Medicare payment policy encourages delaying discharges, a UCLA study concludes

June 8, 2015

Long-term care hospitals — which care for people whose medical conditions require relatively lengthy treatment — are keeping patients longer than necessary because of the way that Medicare determines payment rates, according to a study from the UCLA Fielding School of Public Health.

Public Citizen @Public_Citizen
Incarceration rates (per 100K):

- 🇮🇸 38
- ⚪ 45
- 🇸🇪 57
- ✚ 57
- 🇩🇰 59
- 🇫🇮 59
- 🇸🇮 74
- 🇳🇴 74
- 🇩🇪 78
- 🇮🇹 81
- 🇨🇭 82
- 🇬🇷 93
- 🇦🇹 94
- 🇧🇪 94
- 🇫🇷 96
- 🇳🇱 102
- 🇰🇷 114
- 🇨🇦 114
- 🇱🇺 115
- 🇪🇸 126
- 🇮🇪 129
- 🇲🇹 165
- 🇦🇺 167
- 🇭🇺 184
- 🇰🇿 188
- 🇵🇱 199
- 🇪🇪 202
- 🇹🇭 209
- 🇹🇴 220
- 🇨🇱 233
- 🇺🇾 265
- 🇹🇷 287
- ...
- 🇺🇸 655

Healthcare Insurance Costs   Nursing Homes   Prison System
Detention Centers = $130 - 775 per head/per day
Some corporations abuse the system for astronomical profit

Authorities: $1B Medicare fraud nursing home scam, 3 charged
https://www.foxnews.com › authorities-1b-medicare-fraud-nursing-home-sca...
Jul 22, 2016 - Three people have been charged in an unprecedented $1 billion health care fraud **scam**, accused of using dozens of Miami **nursing homes** to bilk the taxpayer-funded Medicare and Medicaid programs, according to an indictment unsealed Friday. ... All of this was done with little regard for ...

NUMBER OF PEOPLE WHO GO BANKRUPT EVERY YEAR BECAUSE OF MEDICAL BILLS

BRITAIN	0
FRANCE	0
JAPAN	0
GERMANY	0
CANADA	0
NETHERLANDS	0
SWITZERLAND	0
USA	**643,000**

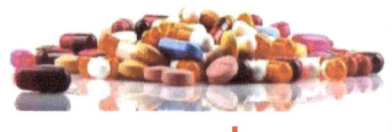

Skyrocketing Drug Prices: What's Driving Up Costs ...
https://accessiblemeds.org › resources › blog › skyrocketing-drug-prices-w... ▼
But when **drug** prices are too high, access to medicines becomes out of reach for far too many patients. ... With brand-name drugs now accounting for 77 percent of all spending on prescription drugs, patients are experiencing higher pharmacy **costs**, higher premiums and

" *This is an issue that affects everyone. From the cities, to rural communities, farmers and ranchers are no exception to high prescription drug prices. In fact, it's actually harder for rural residents to find affordable prescription drugs. Rural Americans face access troubles to quality healthcare, and pharmacies, that compounds the issue.* "

United States has one of the highest **costs** of **healthcare** in the world. In 2017, the **U.S.** spent about $3.5 trillion on **healthcare**, which averages to about $11,000 per person.   Mar 15, 2019

FUN FACT

Healthcare Costs 1960 – 2020
(In Billions)

Year	Cost
1960	$27
1970	$75
1980	$256
1990	$724
2000	$1,377
2010	$2,594
2020P	$4,487

Centers for Medicare and Medicaid Services 2012 California Healthcare Foundation

People Product Pate

Ingredients

- 1 lb Portobello Mushrooms
- 1/2 Tbsp Vegetable Oil
- 1 Tbsp Shallots, chopped
- 4 Thyme Sprigs
- 8 oz Tofu
- 1/2 cup Garbanzo Beans
- 1/2 C canned White Beans
- 1/3 C Bread Crumbs
- 1 Tbsp Soy Sauce
- 1/2 tsp Salt

I know what you are thinking... 'Soylent Green'
Enjoy this tasty pate ...as long as you don't know whats in it.

Directions

Preheat the oven to 400 F (204 C). Transfer the Portobello mushrooms into a large colander. Gently rinse with cold water and drain well. Cut the mushrooms into chunks or simply quarter each one.
Transfer the mushrooms into a large baking pan. Spread everything out, making an even layer. Drizzle with vegetable oil. Sprinkle with 1/8 tsp salt and ground black pepper and the chopped shallots.
Bake in the oven for 10 minutes. Remove from the oven and let cool for 15 minutes.
Remove the leaves from the fresh thyme. Cut the tofu into small cubes. Transfer the garbanzo beans and white beans into a small colander. Wash off the canning liquid by rinsing with cold water. Toss the beans in the colander a few times to remove the excess water. In a large food processor, add the beans, tofu cubes, roasted mushrooms, bread crumbs, thyme leaves, soy sauce, 1/4 tsp ground black pepper and 1/2 tsp salt. Process for 30 seconds. Stir the mixture. Process for another 30 seconds. Repeat this cycle again for pate with medium texture. The total processing time is 2 minutes. For pate with silkier more mousse-like texture, process at intervals for a total of 3 minutes or more. Brush vegetable oil into 4 (8 oz) ramekins, coating the inside completely. Spoon the pate into the ramekins filling each about 3/4 full. Use a spoon or spatula to smooth out the top.

Privately Owned Prisons, Medical Facilities are Profiting Off Prisoners & Patients with Tax Payer Money

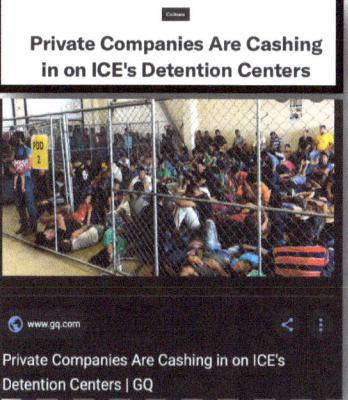

Republicans continue to capture, separate and hold desperate asylum seekers (men, women and children) in detention centers around the country while billing the US tax payers up to $775 per head, per day while the US incarcerates far more prisoners than any other country (per capita).

Democrats are appalled at huge healthcare costs, the in-humane treatment and conditions witnessed at the detention centers and want the Republicans to be held accountable for the huge amount of money being paid to the centers while the detainees complain of having very little access to beds, showers, medical needs or even toothbrushes.

Global Shift Surprise

The World Protests!

Climate-Change Protests Around ...

otested around the globe for ...

Massive Donald Trump protest
mirror.co.uk

meet as Amazon burns and the ...
ost.com

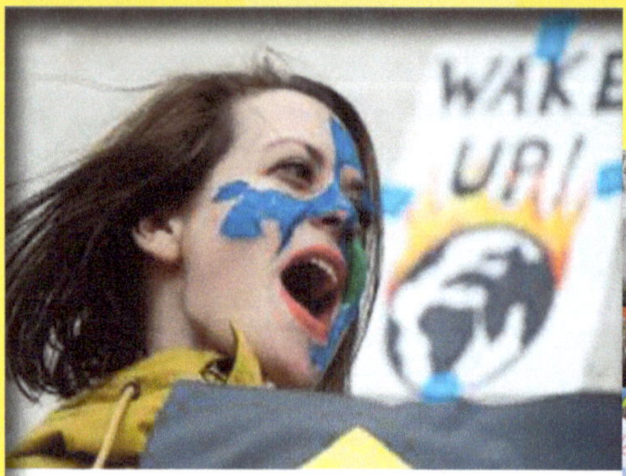

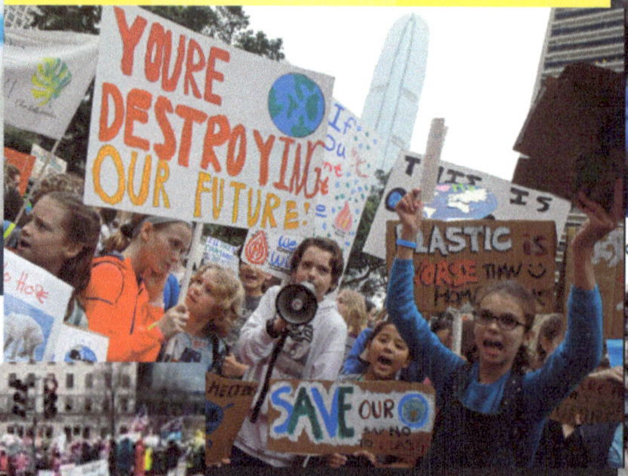

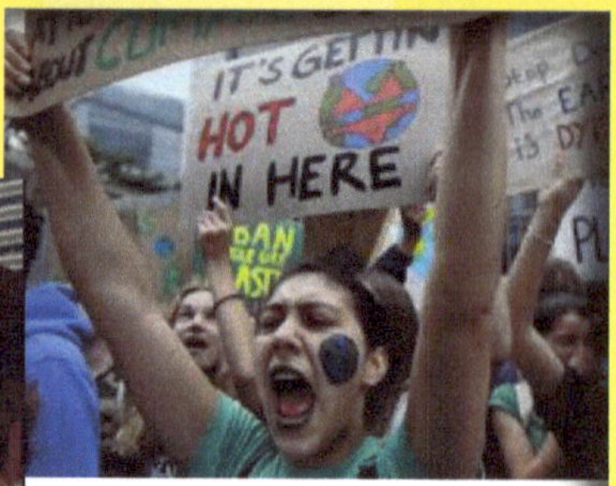

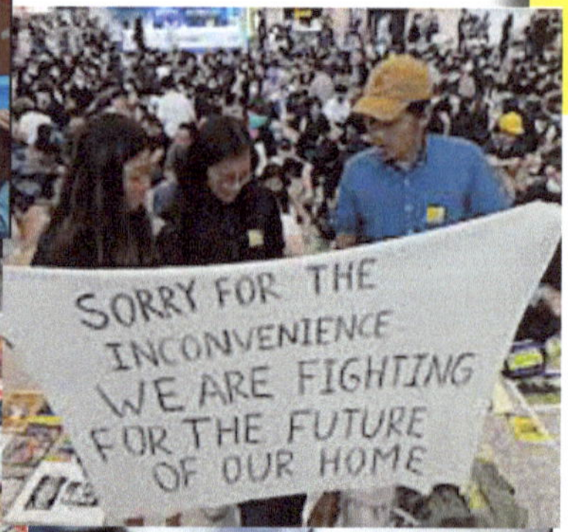

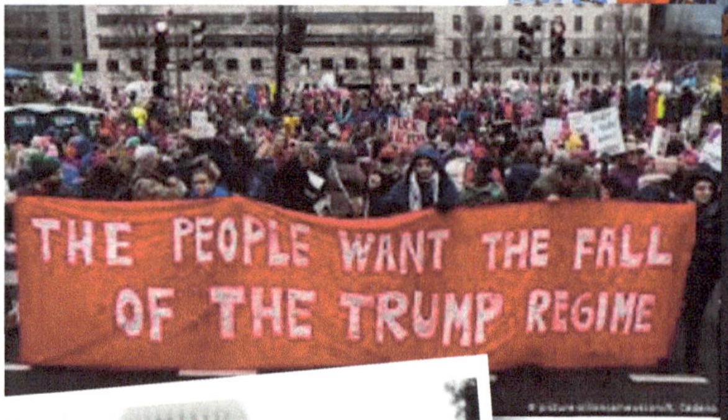

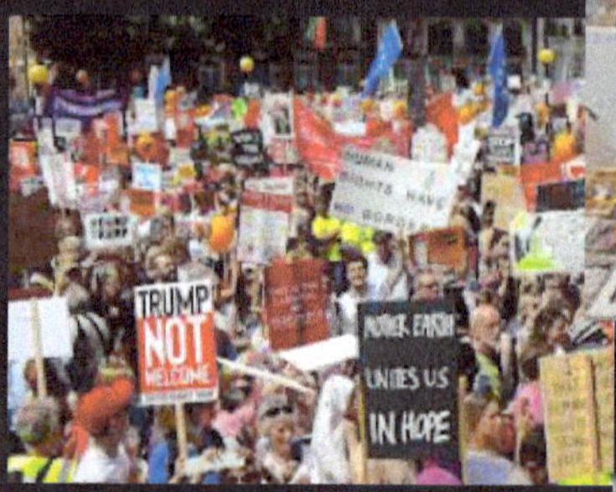

From the Amazon to Hong Kong, Global Protests Rock the World with Record Turn Out.

Portugal - Youth climate strike ...

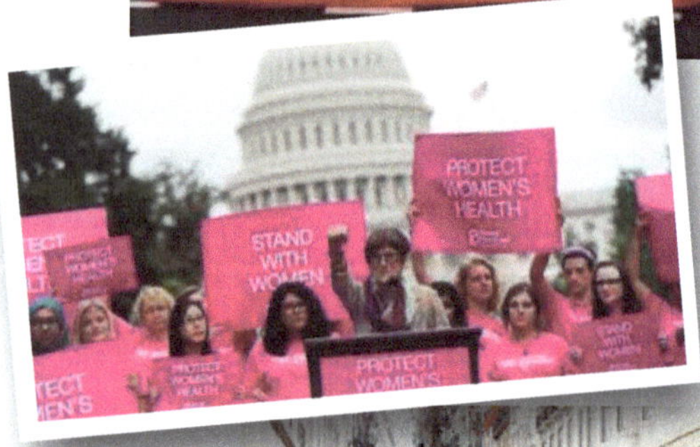

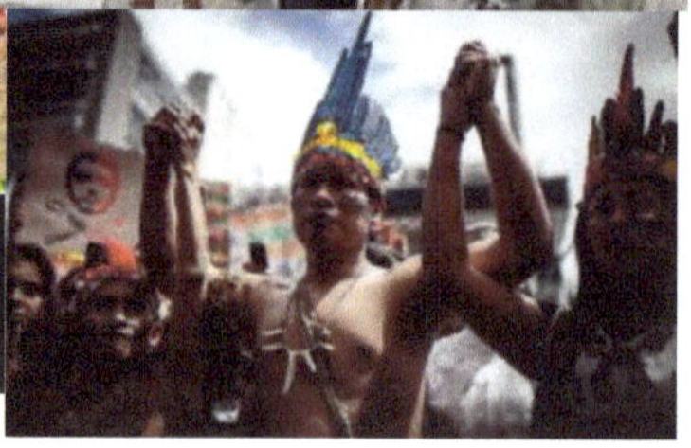

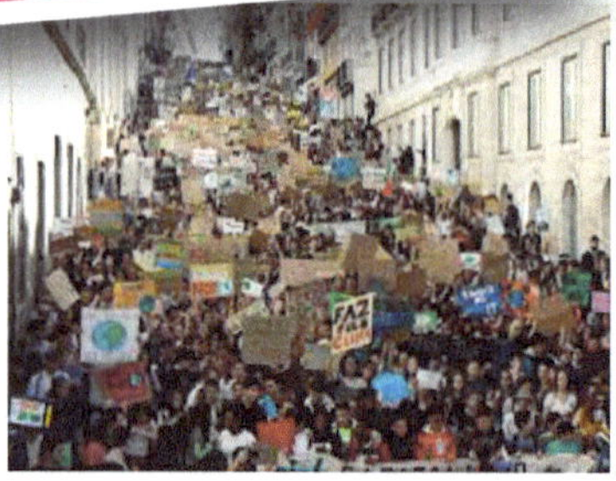

Protesters Came Prepared and Numbered in the Millions

Hong Kong protests erupt into violence as demonstrators defy police ban cbsn.ws/2O3fMuP

Hong Kong Protests: How Did We Get Here ...
thediplomat.com

Hong Kong Free Press @HongKongFP · 9h
Hong Kong's MTR, banks and malls close down after mask ban sparks city-wide unrest hongkongfp.com/2019/10/05/hon... #hongkong #hongkongprotests #antiELAB #china

Hong Kong's MTR, banks and malls close down after mask ban sparks ...
The streets of Hong Kong were quiet on Saturday morning as dozens of shopping malls and banks closed their doors and MTR services ...
hongkongfp.com

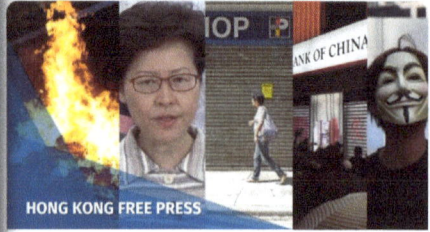

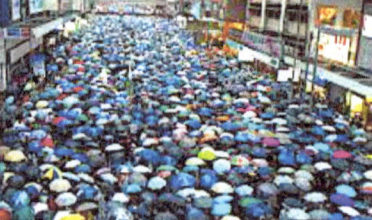

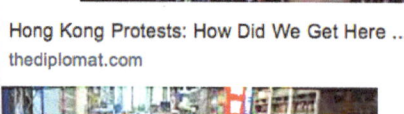

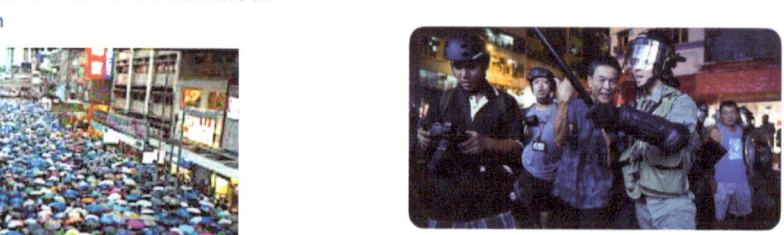

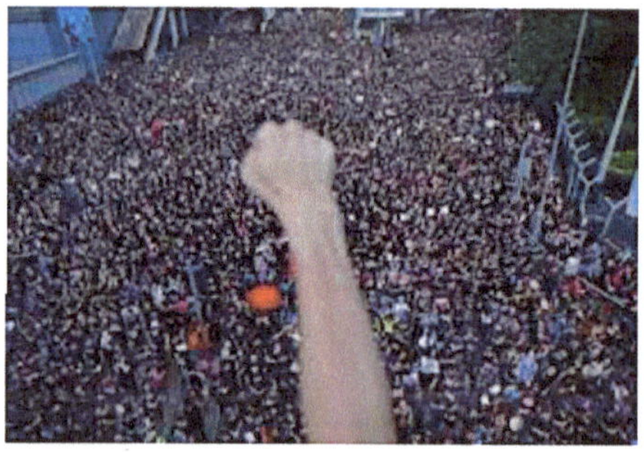

2:39 PM · 9/15/19 · Sprinklr

Global Shift Surprise

Ingredients

1 Pkg Quinoa Fried Rice
1 Egg
1/2 Onion, diced
2 C Broccoli Crowns
1 Carrot, diced
1 Bell Pepper
Soy Sauce, to taste

Leftover Salmon, Chicken or what have you

Enjoy this international dish that is full of surprises.

Directions

Scramble egg in a thin layer of olive oil. Remove and set aside. Toss in veggies and saute' just until tender (don't over cook). Add whatever leftover meats you may have if desired. Add fried rice, a splash of soy sauce and be surprised how good and satisfying this tasty little dish is.

All over the world protesters risked life and limb to fight for rights and climate change action.

1,000 anti-Putin protesters arrested as ...
metro.co.uk

BBC NEWS

Russia protests: Thousand arrests at Moscow rally

Republicans condemn liberal protesters and believe they are just sore losers and "snowflakes."

Democrats are furious about having to defend womens' rights, healthcare costs, cuts to FEMA, the FDA and EPA, the lack of climate change action and the tripling deficit. They are also outraged at the lack of immigration policy and processing (separated kids in cages, etc.) and unchecked corruption.

Berry Bonkers

Now that it looks like Deutsche Bank disappeared Trump's tax returns and scrubbed its servers, it seems like an appropriate moment to mention that Trump's "special banker" at Deutsche was Justice Kennedy's son (not mentioned in this recent news).

FUN FACT

BREAKING: US scrambled to get a top spy out of Russia after Trump revealed highly classified info -

FUN FACT

2020 presidential campaign .

Deutsche Bank may have destroyed copies of Trump's tax returns, cle...
The bank told a federal appeals court that it no longer holds records of President Donald Trump's tax returns.
🔗 newsweek.com

New York Daily News @NYDailyNews Follow

The big story at @FoxNews today isn't Paul Manafort's indictment — it's the "emoji cheeseburger crisis" nydn.us/2zjLb5w

Politics The Wrap
Trump Suggests That Congress Investigate Obama's 'Ridiculous Netflix Deal'
President Donald Trump on Monday suggested that the House Judiciary Committee should redirect its efforts from questions about his own busines...

Long-Standing White House Press Briefings have been stopped since mid-2019. Reporters clammer to gain information from the President himself when he walks to the WH Chopper. 'Chopper Talk' a lot of noise, yelling and ditched questions.

World Business Insider
Trump keeps threatening US enemies with destructive power greater than nuclear weapons -...
Nothing comes close to a thermonuclear weapon. Insider spoke to the US's leading arms control experts, who struggled to make sense of what Trump...

 Real Angry Boomer ☮ 🆘
@realangryboomer

Maybe each state should become a country.

📰 The New York Times
'Trump Unplugged': A President as His Own National Security Adviser
President Trump is now free to command his foreign policy after dumping John R. Bolton, the last major internal counterweight to his dealings ...

 🆘 **SCOOT** 🆘 @Scoot4002 · 1h
Fuck it everyone gets walls
#ColoradoBorderWall 👷 🤣

A Response to Trump's Colorado Border Wall Statement ...And Who's Gonna Pay For It? New Mexico, I presume...

112

"His mood changes from one minute to the next, based on a headline or tweet, next thing you know, his entire schedule gets tossed out the window *because he's losing his s---*

- former WH official with anonymity: internal conversations about the Pres.

Donald Trump has said he knows who was behind the al-Qaeda terror attacks on the US in September 2001 and added that "Iraq did not knock down the World Trade Centre".

"It was not Iraq," the president told ABC News. "It were other people. And I think I know who the other people were. And you might also."

Berry Bonkers

Ingredients

Pomegranate-Blueberry Juice
Cherry Seltzer Water
Blueberry Vodka
Ice Cubes

Flower Petals, Cherries,
Blueberries, whatever
(Snapdragon, Pansy,
Lavender, Mint)

Enjoy the Colorful and Flavorful Berry Bonkers ...you're gonna need it!

Directions

Pour the vodka over ice cubes.
Splash in the pomegranate/Blueberry juice and mix in a big splash of cherry seltzer water. Stir.
Top with whatever your little heart desires.

ElizabethR @ElizabethRBess · Nov 10, 2018
FOX STATE TV hasn't tweeted in 2 days. Rumor has it it's in protest of what happened to Tucker Carlson, but no one really knows. I'm praying it's permanent!

FUN FACT The FOX twitter feed was innodated with Liberal rebuttals prior to their 'going dark' for unknown reasons.

what was his first clue? The gluttony, the sloth, vainglory, wrath, greed, anger, covetousness or lust that includes illicit sexual desire?

Pope Says Trump 'Is Not Christian'
npr.org

More Mass Shootings, More "Thoughts & Prayers"

Some may think things are a little 'Bonkers' these days, while others couldn't be more pleased.....and THAT, my friend, is at the heart of Bonkersville.

Kellyanne introduces an "alternative Constitution".
Kellyanne Conway: It's unconstitutional for Democrats to 'embarrass this president' with impeachment -

And Heeeere's Rudy...

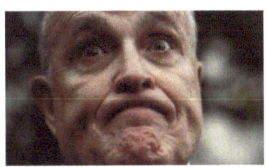
Rudy Giuliani a Subject of Criminal ...

Kellyanne Conway: It's unconstitutional for Democrats to 'embarrass this presi...
White House aide Kellyanne Conway on Sunday insisted that Democrats do not have a "constitutional basis" to embarrass President Donald Trump by ...
rawstory.com

Republicans are OK with Rudy Giuliani working without clearance, 'behind the scenes' while US Ambassadors play by the rules. They are also OK with Trump obstructing justice by demanding key Republican witnesses ignore federal subpoenas..."But look at the ECONOMY!"

Democrats are happy to reach for a Berry Bonkers. After about a half a dozen, they relax and reflect on saner times when Presidents didn't believe Putin over US Intel and get "Love Letters" from brutal Dictators.

Very Berry Bonkers

MY PERSONAL ATTORNEY IS CURRENTLY UNDER CRIMINAL INVESTIGATION

NOT TO BE CONFUSED WITH MY FORMER ATTORNEY WHO IS CURRENTLY IN PRISON **FUN FACT**

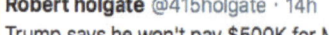

Robert holgate @415holgate · 14h
Trump says he won't pay $500K for MN rally. He still owes DC $9M.

Trump faces blistering criticism at ...
timesofisrael.com

Trump says he won't pay $500K for MN rally. He still owes DC $9M.
President Donald Trump took to Twitter Tuesday to accuse the mayor of Minneapolis of trying to "stifle free speech" over the city's $530,000 b...

McConnell blocks two election security bills

BY JORDAIN CARNEY - 07/25/19 01:13 PM EDT

"Civil War 2" trends on Twitter after Trump quotes speculation that impeachment would spark "civil war"

Entertainment The Wrap
Sean Spicer's 'Dancing With the Stars' Debut Draws Stunned Reactions: 'I Can't Believe This'
Former White House press secretary Sean Spicer took to the "Dancing With the Stars" stage Monday night for the first time, wearing a bright yellow to...

FUN FACT

Shoot Migrants' Legs, Build Alligator Moat: Behind Trump's ...
https://www.nytimes.com › 2019/10/01 › politics › trump-border-wars
2 days ago - [Update: **Trump** denies considering a border **moat**.] ... about fortifying a border wall with a water-filled trench, stocked with **snakes** or alligators, ...

Trump calls for extension of term limits for key politicians
After a wave of retirements, the president plans to do away with the party's six-year limit on how long politicians can serve as chairs.
'It is a better way to go' »

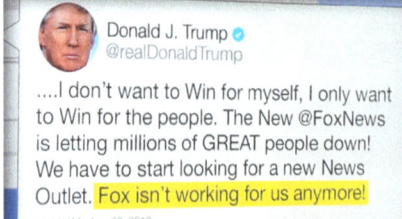

Donald J. Trump
@realDonaldTrump

....I don't want to Win for myself, I only want to Win for the people. The New @FoxNews is letting millions of GREAT people down! We have to start looking for a new News Outlet. Fox isn't working for us anymore!
10:03 AM - Aug 28, 2019

Dems hunt.
Dems were in the military.
Dems own guns.

Patriots have more people ready to fight to save our country than nationalists have to divide it.

FUN FACT

NBCNews.com
Rudy Giuliani butt-dials NBC reporter, heard discussing need for cash and trashing Bidens
Late in the night Oct. 16, Rudy Giuliani made a phone call to this reporter. The fact that Giuliani was reaching out wasn't remarkable. He and the ...
Oct 25, 2019

Very Berry Bonkers

Ingredients

- Pomegranate-Blueberry Juice
- Cherry Seltzer Water
- Blueberry Vodka
- Ice Cubes
- Flower Petals, Cherries, Blueberries, whatever (Snapdragon, Pansy, Lavender, Mint)

Things are so bonkers, you might want an extra Berry Bonkers to take the edge off...

Directions

Pour the vodka over ice cubes...(same stuff, just add more than the basic bankers)
Splash in the pomegranate/Blueberry juice and mix in another splash of cherry seltzer water. Stir.
Top with whatever your little heart desires, because nothing seems to matter anyway...

> **Tony Posnanski** @tonyposnanski · Oct 13
> I don't know who needs to hear this right now, but Fuck Donald Trump, Mike Pence, Gym Jordan, Mitch McConnell, Doug Collins, The Lemonade stand woman, Ann Coulter, Tomi Lahren, Ted Cruz, Matt Gaetz, Scott Baio, Jerry Falwell Jr., Marco Rubio, and every single MAGA motherfucker.

Barbara Malmet @B52Malmet · 9m
Under Trump, many of the political appointees "have absolutely no understanding of U.S. government policy and State Department policy. They don't know what the hell they're doing," one former U.S. ambassador said. Wait till Sondland is deposed Thursday.

Polo ponies and private planes: Trump impeachment fight deepens a rift among ambassadors
🔗 politico.com

Shannon Watts @sh... · 1d
When gently corrected by one of the astronauts about how other women have spacewalked, Donald Trump uses his middle finger to "fix" his hair.

How is this even real life?

Is Rudy Giuliani Losing His Mind ...
politico.com

Eric Trump bashes the children of politicians profiting off their family name to enrich themselves: 'It is sickening' -

Eric Trump bashes the children of politicians profiting off their family...
rawstory.com

4:31 AM · 10/20/19 · Twitter Web Client

Republicans continue to rally around their leader no matter what he does or says. Most don't 'tune-in' to current events reported by reputable news outlets and when/if they do hear something that seems 'Bonkers,' they attribute it to "Fake News."

Democrats reach for another Very Berry Bonkers and wonder what kind of people could think this stuff is OK.

Meanwhile Mojitos

TECH & SCIENCE

China Is About to Fire Up Its 'Artificial Sun' in Quest for Fusion Energy

It is hoped the nuclear fusion device will help scientists overcome a key problem in harnessing plasma inside tokamaks.

TECH & SCIENCE

Artificial Flowers That Bend Toward Light and Harvest Solar Energy Created

Researchers say their SunBOTs are 400 percent more efficient than comparable stationary devices.

ACTIVE VOLCANOES AROUND THE WORLD THAT COULD ERUPT AT ANY MOMENT

BY **LAURA POWERS** ON 12/13/19 AT 8:25 AM EST

Despite the dangers, tourists continue to flock to these volatile places for incredible views and to take a peek at Mother Nature's temperamental hotspots.

Hero pic erupting volcano
TRUECAPTURE/GETTY

TECH & SCIENCE

Scientists Say They'll Plant 1 Billion Trees by 2028 Using Drones

Earth loses 13 billion trees per year but regains less than half.

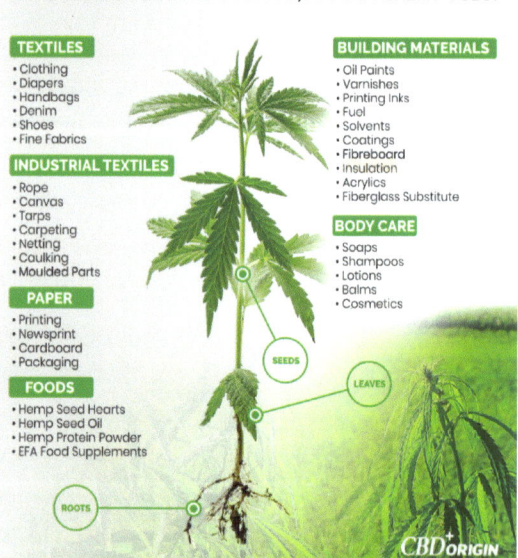

TECH & SCIENCE

TikTok Has Been Banned From Government-Issued Cell Phones by the U.S. Navy

The Chinese owned application, which is viewed with suspicion by some U.S. politicians, has been deemed unsafe by top officials at the Navy - but it remains unclear just what the dangers may be.

TECH & SCIENCE

2,000-foot-wide Asteroid to Speed Past the Earth Just After Christmas

The asteroid will travel past our planet at a staggering velocity of around 27,500 miles per hour.

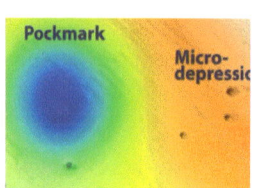

TECH & SCIENCE

Thousands of Mysterious Holes Discovered on Seafloor Off California Coast

It is unclear how the holes were formed, although marine trash could partly be responsible.

TECH & SCIENCE

Breast Cancer Linked to Permanent Hair Dye and Chemical Hair Straighteners

A study based on the medical records of more than 45,000 women found a positive correlation between permanent hair dye and breast cancer—particularly among those who are black.

116

Meanwhile Mojitos

Ingredients

- Silver Rum
- Fresh Mint Leaves
- Green Tea Powder
- 1 Lime, sliced
- Agave or Mint Stevia
- Club Soda
- Lots of Ice Cubes

Meanwhile, there are a lot of things happening in the world and some of them are actually good!

Directions

Place mint leaves and 1 lime wedge into a sturdy glass. Use a muddler to crush the mint, tea and lime. Add 2 more lime wedges and the sweetener, muddle again to release the lime juice. Do not strain the mixture. Fill the glass almost to the top with ice. Pour the rum over the ice, and fill the glass with club soda. Garnish with the remaining lime wedge and mint leaves.

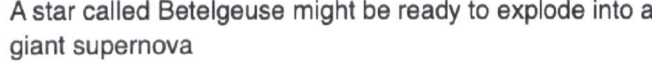

MIT Technology Review

A star called Betelgeuse might be ready to explode into a giant supernova

Betelgeuse is one of the brightest stars in the night sky, but it's fainter than it's been in nearly a century, dimming by a factor of two since just...

5 days ago

TECH & SCIENCE

This Artificial Neuron Could One Day Be Used to Treat Chronic Conditions

Researchers describe the process that enabled them to make artificial equivalents of two types of neurons—hippocampal and respiratory. They hope that one day it could help treat people with damaged neurons.

Everything from Green Mojitos to Running Robots—There is A Lot Going On Out There!

TECH & SCIENCE

Music Is Universal, Used in 'Strikingly Similar Ways' Across the Globe

Researchers spent five years painstakingly creating a database which features music created by people around the world.

How Boston Dynamics Is Redefin...
spectrum.ieee.org

Republicans are OK with Mojitos

Democrats think Mojitos are OK

Whistleblower Tea

Whistleblower

A whistleblower is a person who exposes secretive information or activity that is deemed illegal, unethical, or not correct within a private or public organization. Wikipedia

Many people who witness wrong doing say nothing for fear of retaliations

Trump demands whistleblower be identified and testify

New York Post
5 hours ago

CNN
90 former national security officials praise whistleblower
Washington (CNN) Ninety former US national security officials wrote a letter Sunday praising the anonymous whistleblower whose recent ...

Michael Cohen, Though Technically Not A Whistle Blower, Says He Wants To Tell What He Knows About Trump.

Michael Cohen Just Started a Process ...

Trump and GOP Call to ID Whistleblower Exposes Glaring Gaps in Protections

Lindsey Graham Says He'll Out Whistleblowers If Trump Is Impeached essence.com/news/lindsey-g.. via @ESSENCE

Trump Orders Cut to National Security Staff After Whistle-Blower 🚨😳
OMG! This guy is destroying our National Security 😱

FUN FACT

Trump Orders Cut to National Security Staff After Whistle-Blower
President Donald Trump has ordered a substantial reduction in the staff of the National Security Council, according to five people familiar with ...
bloomberg.com

The Washington Post @washingtonpost · 1h
Trump calls for ending the impeachment inquiry, says whistleblower should be "exposed"

Whistleblower Tea

Ingredients

- Water
- Green Tea Powder
- Mint Sprig
- Ginger
- Honey

Directions

Relax with some nice whistle blowing tea. Feel good about doing the right thing, but watch your back! .

Boil some fresh clean water in an old-fashioned tea kettle (or a miccrowave and whistle along). Grab your favorite mug, pour hot water and add the green tea powder, ginger slice, sweetener and mint sprig. Enjoy the sweet bite of self-righteousness. No, no, it's OK. You did the right thing. Really, you did.

Jailed Trump fixer Michael Cohen says he can't wait to pen post jail tell-all book
Michael Cohen can't wait to get out of prison for obvious reasons: He's ... Intelligence Committee to provide a testimony of his work for Trump.

WHISTLEBLOWER
TRUMP SUGGESTS EXECUTING THE WHISTLE-BLOWER'S SOURCES LIKE "IN THE OLD DAYS"

21 hours ago
Trump Jr. Says Vindman Deserves Attacks ...
politicaldig.com

Newsweek
Who Is Brittany Kaiser? Whistle-blower in Documentary 'The Great Hack'
Netflix documentary The Great Hack, which focuses on the Cambridge Analytica data scandal, includes an exposé of Brittany Kaiser, a former ...

Trump: "I think it's important to find out who the person (Whistleblower) is...."

Cowardly Congressman: mouthes "OK." then hangs his head down.

WHAT THE CRAP?!
#TrumpMinneapolis

Republicans are only concerned about the Bidens and finding out who the 'Whistle-Blower' is, even though several decorated and vetted high-ranking US officials have already corroborated the information.

Democrats want to protect the 'Whistle-Blower' from GOP retaliation and remind the GOP that there are multiple witnesses who have already given similar testimony during the impeachment hearing, making the original whistle-blower's identity irrelevant.

Coup Soup

Coup d'état - Wikipedia
https://en.wikipedia.org › wiki › Coup_d'état ▾

A **coup d'état** (/ˌkuː deɪˈtɑː/ (listen); French: [ku deta]), also known by its German name putsch (/pʊtʃ/), or simply as a **coup**, is the overthrow of an existing government by non-democratic means; typically, it is an illegal, unconstitutional seizure of power by a dictator, the military, or a political faction.

FUN FACT An Impeachment Hearing is Actually the Opposite of a Coup

 Fox News

Trump brands impeachment inquiry a 'coup' as House holds third day of public hearings

Adam Schiff, D-Calif., led a coup that Democrats plotted after his ... the sentiments of millions of people," Zaid told Fox News in November.

 Fox News

Trump campaign accuses Dems of 'coup' in new campaign ad featuring Biden, Schiff, 'Squad'

Lindsey Graham, R-S.C., calling it "based on hearsay." It also focuses on House Intelligence Committee Chairman Rep. Adam Schiff, D-Calif., ...

Oct 2, 2019

Impeachment hearings began in November 2019 The public was able to view the proceedings on TV and Live Social Media Feeds.

Impeachment hearings are being held to investigate the possibility of the Trump Administration's obstruction of congress, extortion, etc., in regard to the withholding of strategic, pre-approved and crucial aid for Ukraine's protection from imminent Russian attacks.

"Do Us A Favor Though"

The GOP disparages a decorated military ...
mercurynews.com

The Mercury News

Letter: If I ignored a subpoena, I'd be in handcuffs within hours

Why is it that everyone in the Trump administration is allowed to ignore a subpoena and not go to jail? If I ignored a subpoena, I'd be in ...

1 month ago

FUN FACT

120

Coup Soup

Ingredients

1 Package Creamy Chicken Soup mix (dry)

Shredded Carrots
Peas

Is Coup Soup a process or a culinary anarchy? Either way, it is delicious!.

Directions

Just follow the directions on the package. There is a process here, but you can ignore it if you want to. You can withhold the main ingredients or add some extra, either way, Coup Soup is delicious.

Trump campaign accuses Dems of 'coup ...
foxnews.com

CNN International

New evidence raises the question: Is Nunes an investigator or participant in Ukraine affair?

Washington (CNN) Rep. Devin Nunes, the top Republican on the House Intelligence Committee, was closer to the central figures in the Ukraine ..

Impeachment hearings are designed to hear testimony of key witnesses to establish the need to proceed with an impeachment of not.

FUN FACT

Key witnesses were subpoenaed, (both Democrats and Republicans) with first-hand knowledge, but the White House blocked key Republican witnesses who were actually on the call or involved with the withholding of the Ukraine aid, from testifying.

- Republicans literally rant (yelling during proceedings) about unfairness of the process because they can't call the Whistleblower (protection laws), Joe or Hunter Biden (irrelevant) to testify. They block witnesses and withhold documents. More winning for Republicans!
- Democrats remain calm and poised to question relevant witnesses that have information, on the Ukraine call/aid, They ask that key Republican witnesses testify, Pompeo, Bolton, Giuliani, Mulvaney and Trump himself.

Integrity Iced Tea

Integrity, Ethics, Honesty, Respect — These four concepts define the strength and value of a nation.

Daniel J. McCarthy @McArtichoke · 6h
WOW: The Lawsuit against McConnell's Obstruction of Judge Garland's Nomination Has Been Refiled

The Lawsuit against McConnell's Obstruction of Judge Garland's Nomi...
New York City [09/03/2019]: On March 16, 2019, Equal Vote America Corp. (EVA) filed a civil lawsuit against Mitch McConnell and Charles ...
dailykos.com

Politics MarketWatch
Former Republican unleashes on the 'rotten to the core' politicians of the GOP
David Jolly That's how the former Florida congressman and self-proclaimed Never-Trumper answered the question,...

HuffPost ✓ @HuffPost · 8m
Senate Republicans just confirmed Justin Walker, 37, to be a lifetime federal judge, even though he was rated "not qualified" by the American Bar Association.

Trump sold a $40 million estate to a Russian oligarch for $100 million—and a senator wants to know why

Trump sold a $40 million estate to a Russian oligarch for $100 million—...
newsweek.com

10:10 PM · 9/1/19 · Twitter Web Client

INTEGRITY
CHOOSING YOUR THOUGHTS AND ACTIONS BASED ON VALUES RATHER THAN PERSONAL GAIN

Integrity
(in-teg'ri-tē) n.
1. Having the character quality of being honest, reliable and fair.

Senate Confirms Another Trump Court Pick Rated 'N...
huffpost.com

Republican groups pressing Sen. Collins as impeachment trial nears - Collins:"I take seriously the oath I will swear to render 'impartial justice' in the impeachment trial. Threats from both the left and the right will have zero influence on my decisions."

Republican groups pressing Sen. Collins as impeachme...
pressherald.com

Tammy H #Resist #Bluetsu...
@tmbeanie415

And it's amazing how the @GOP just turn a blind eye to everything he does, or makes excuses for the lies he tells. It's just sickening the way this administration just plays blind and stupid. It's time to just vote every @GOP out and never vote them back in again. Accountability! twitter.com/

Amee Vanderpool @girlsreallyrule · 2h
As Marie Yovanovitch departs the audience in the gallery breaks into applause and some give her a standing ovation because she has more than earned it.

From CSPAN ✓

Integrity Iced Tea

Ingredients

Lots of Ice
1 Shot Vodka
1 Shot Spiced Rum

Splash of Dr Pepper
Mint Sprig

Integrity is suffering these days. Salute the good ones and ease the pain with a nice, tall, Integrity Iced Tea

Directions

Measure it right. Don't cheat, Mix it all together and enjoy.

 Native American Wisdom @NativeAmWisdom · 1m
Truth, acceptance of the truth, is a shattering experience. It shatters the binding shroud of culture trance. It rips apart smugness, arrogance, superiority, and self-importance.
— Paula Gunn Allen

NativeAmerican wisdom quotes

VF Vanity Fair

Wildly Incriminating Emails Show the White House Knew Trump Was Extorting Ukraine

Staff, including Mick Mulvaney, scrambled to justify the hold on nearly $400 million in aid in exchange for investigations.

Politics HuffPost
National Security Council's Alexander Vindman Told To Keep Quiet About Trump...

No hard feelings, Nationals fans: Trump to host winning World Series team at White House USA TODAY

Trump says he wants Ukraine's President Zelenskiy to visit the White House Reuters

Republicans have no problem with withholding needed (congress approved) aid to get dirt on Hunter Biden (who is a private US citizen). Their main goal is to expose the whistleblower.

Democrats believe Trump is incompetent and should be removed from office—a danger to national security, the economy and society. Dems maintain integrity standards and ethics during the process.

Testify Teriyaki

CNBC
House Democrats' impeachment report accuses Trump of obstruction, other misconduct

Mulvaney has refused to comply with a House subpoena for his testimony ... and Agencies to Ignore Subpoenas for Documents and Testimony.

"IT WAS A PERFECT CALL!"

"NO QUID PRO QUO!"

~ Donald J Trump

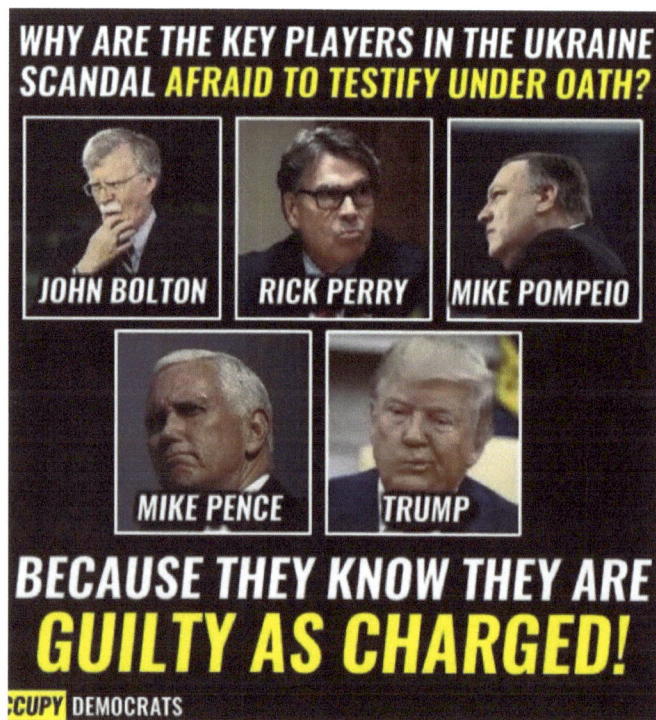

Testify Teriyaki

Ingredients

Fresh Salmon Fillet
Olive Oil
Paprika

Garlic Powder
Chill Powder
Cayenne Pepper

Enjoy the succulent side of Testify Teriyaki Salmon. It's been a long day

Directions

Rinse Salmon and place on baking dish with light a coat of olive oil on both sides. Sprinkle seasons on both sides and bake at 385° for approximately 15 minutes.

Democrats invite key players with first-hand knowledge to testify, including but not limited to; Trump, Guilliani, Pompeo, Bolton and Mulvaney—All of which refuse to testify (as of Dec 2019)

FUN FACT Politico

PENCE KNEW

Senate Dems ask that Mick Mulvaney and John Bolton testify ...

Those requests would seem to ignore Trump's preferred witnesses. ... Schumer also proposes "that the Senate issue subpoenas for a limited ...

The Hill

Schiff knocks Mulvaney over failure to testify in impeachment probe | TheHill

Schiff in a statement also condemned Mulvaney for working "to block others from complying with subpoenas" and not giving Congress ...

Republicans complain about the "process" but block Republican witnesses directly involved. They also demand that the Whistleblower testify, even though several high ranking officials have corroborated the story and the Whistle Blower is protected by law.

Democrats have to decide which 'High Crimes and Misdemeanors' to include in the Articles of Impeachment. They fear that if they list them all, it may confuse people. They chose Obstruction and Abuse of Power.

Law & Order Oatmeal

Law & Order

Law and order is the cornerstone of a successful society. When the citizens see the highest, most respected levels of office committing crimes and 'getting away with it,' it leads to a degradation of social norms. Why follow the rules if cheaters and lairs aren't?

Law & Order Oatmeal

Ingredients

- Instant Oatmeal
- Water
- Walnuts
- Banana
- Cinnamon
- Clove
- Nutmeg

Directions

Start your day with some good 'ol fashioned Law & Order Oatmeal and try to stay on the right side of the law

Yes, its instant, we don't have a lot to waste here. Boil the water, stir into oatmeal, cover for a minute or two - eat up and then go out there and do some lawful good!

Thousands marched to the Capitol yesterday to demand Congress do its job and impeach Trump. Virtually no media covered it.
#wethepeoplemarch

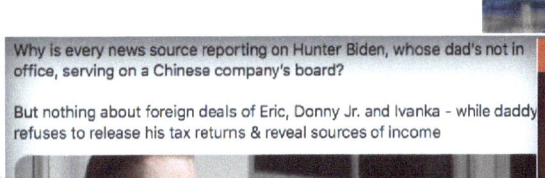

FUN FACT

CNN
GOP challenger Bill Weld: Trump committed treason and 'the penalty for treason ... is death'
Washington (CNN) Former Massachusetts governor and longshot candidate for the GOP nomination for president Bill Weld on Monday ...
19 hours ago

Republicans are noticing some of Trump's ...incidents but most think it's a "Witch Hunt, Soft Coup, and/or Smear Campaign," like they say on FOX news and like what Trump says at his numerous rallies and in his tweets.

Democrats and independent groups are conducting numerous investigations and sticking to the legal system that seems to be moving too slowly and ineffectively. There is heavy frustration felt by many.

Jaw Dropping Justice Juice

BREAKING NEWS
TRUMP BRACING FOR SENATE TRIAL AFTER BEING IMPEACHED

politics
House votes to formalize impeachment inquiry procedures

Clare Foran, Jeremy Herb, Alex Rogers and Haley Byrd, CNN

Updated 11:46 AM EDT October 31, 2019
Washington

 **GOP** @GOP

Nancy Pelosi's announcement to proceed with articles of impeachment directly contradicts the will of the American people.

This impeachment sham is purely political-- which is why Democrats are rushing the process & putting KEY legislative items like the USMCA on the back burner.

9:09 AM · Dec 5, 2019 · Sprout Social

The Big Dead One @CthulhuRules · 1h
Replying to @GOP
It does NOT contradict the will of the American people. The majority want him gone. The majority did NOT want him. We the People have had ENOUGH!
#ImpeachAndRemoveTrump
#NotMyPresident

CNN @CNN · 8h
These five surprising moments from the Trump impeachment inquiry changed the course of the investigation

5 surprises from the impeachment inquiry
The impeachment inquiry into President Donald Trump has had it all: Contentious public hearings, unexpected bombshells and a fair share ...
cnn.com

Josh Marshall @joshtpm · 18h
This - FINALLY - is the point. Very, very clear that the White House finally released the aid only when the whistleblower report was coming to light and the Intel committee was already starting its investigation! They relented because they finally got caught.

Los Angeles Times
Letters to the Editor: The founders did not foresee a party that would protect a demagogue

 MusingsofaMisanthrope @MusingMsAnthrop · 1s
Replying to @ABC
Republicans had hearings for Clinton over messing around with an intern. Trump has been accused of rape (52 cases?), has committed numerous national security risks, dozens of law suits for criminal behavior but MAGAts can't comprehend the need for this impeachment process.

Jaw Dropping Justice Juice

Ingredients

6 oz Pineapple Juice or Apple Juice
1 banana
1 C Baby Spinach
1 Carrot

6 Ice Cubes
1/2 Tbsp Green Tea Powder
1/2 tsp Ginger (ground)
Honey or Agave (to taste)

Let your jaw hit the floor as you watch all the investigations and proceedings

Directions

Get all the relevant ingredients together, throw them in the blender and see how it comes out.

"Read The Transcript!" They Did...

FUN FACT

"A PRESIDENT WHO DOESN'T COMPLY WITH CONGRESSIONAL REQUESTS FOR INFORMATION IS SUBJECT TO IMPEACHMENT." — LINDSEY GRAHAM, 1998
Lindsey Graham, 1998
During Clinton Impeachment Hearings

David Brooks: Taylor's Testimony Was "The Smoking Gun," "Seals The Deal"

"Thoughts & Prayers"

Pentagon & Congress
Pentagon told witness not to testify in Trump impeachment inquiry
By: Eric Tucker, The Associated Press

Pelosi, Schiff Ramp Up Impeachment ...
usnews.com

Republicans complain about "the process." The White House has blocked key witnesses, refused to submit documents and ignored federal subpoenas. Republicans demand Joe and Hunter Biden testify.
Note: The Bidens have no interaction or information about the Ukraine call

Democrats and Republicans can agree on this one thing—Democrats are not "street-fighters." Many have become frustrated at the lack of 'push-back' towards Republican corruption and scandal...until now.

Impeachment Pouch

With those 10 words, Donald Trump triggered the investigation that would lead him to become the third impeached president in U.S.

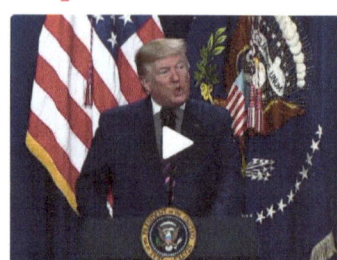

FOX NEWS
House Dems raise prospect of new impeachment articles, in court battle over McGahn testimony
2h ago

Schiff presided over the impeachment hearing and delivered passionate and poignant speeches that moved Democrats.

House managers deliver articles of nbcnews.com

Testimony of decorated veterans and high ranking officials corroborated whisltleblower statements

Chip Franklin @chipf... · 1d
You have two choices; a lying sociopath or American heroes. Just kidding, there's only one choice. #RemoveTrumpNow

The impeachment hearing was televised LIVE nationally and globally.

FUN FACT Other Trump Related Entires Are Still Under Investigations.

Replying to @CBSNews
It is as if he WANTS to be impeached. He's probably saying, "What the hell do I have to do to get out of this gig, without Putin thinking I quit?!?!?"
8:29 PM · Sep 7, 2019 · Twitter for iPhone

Josh Marshall @joshtpm · 18h
This - FINALLY - is the point. Very, very clear that the White House finally released the aid only when the whistleblower report was coming to light and the Intel committee was already starting its investigation! They relented because they finally got caught.

Impeachment Pouch

Ingredients

- Pita Bread
- 1 Pkg Veggie Crumbles
- 1 Red Bell Pepper
- Red Onion
- Shredded Cheese
- Mayonnaise

Keep your energy up as you enjoy an Impeachment Pouch Surprise. It's surprisingly delicious!

Directions

Slice the red peppers into thin strips and dice the red onion. Heat veggie crumbles in pan or skillet (medium heat). Push to the outside and heat peppers and onion until slightly tender. Mix together and heat another 2 minutes. Place pita bread on top while skillet is still warm for a minute or two. Tear pita bread in half and coat inside with mayonnaise. Stuff the veggies and veggie crumbles into each pouch and top with shredded cheese.

Sarah Kendzior @sarahkendzior · 55m
If reporters feel the impeachment hearings aren't "exciting" enough, they can go report on Trump's decades of mafia ties, sexual assaults, financial crimes, and all the other horrifying activity they failed to cover

Josh Jordan @NumbersMuncher · 1h
GOP: Trump never asked Ukraine to investigate the Bidens.

Trump: I totally did.

GOP: But it wasn't a quid pro quo at least!

Kyle Clark @KyleClark · 9m
Colorado talk radio host Chuck Bonniwell of @710KNUS said he wished for "a nice school shooting" to interrupt coverage of President Trump's impeachment. #copolitics #9NEWS

Donald J. Trump IMPEACHED on December 18, 2019 Henceforth known as #IMPOTUS

"It Was A Perfect Call!"

- Republicans claim the impeachment hearings are unfair and have no basis. They complain the process is going too fast and that is going too slow as well. They claim the "Democrats have no case" and they continue to try to "get dirt on Hunter Binden."

- Democrats passed two Articles of Impeachment through the House. They are currently preparing for an Impeachment Trial in the Republican majority senate. They want agreed upon rules, before trial begins.

Fascist Fricassee

Fascism

Fascism is a form of far-right, authoritarian ultranationalism characterized by dictatorial power, forcible suppression of opposition, and strong regimentation of society and of the economy which came to prominence in early 20th-century Europe.
Wikipedia

Conservative Denver radio station 710 KNUS fired host and former district attorney Craig Silverman during his broadcast Saturday after he criticized Donald Trump, according to the Denver Post.

Some Examples of Fascism:

Harassing, beating and arresting peaceful protesters and those not of a particular party, ethnicity, religion, ideology is a form of fascism. Terminating honorable government officials who stand in the way of corruption, ignoring 'due process,' blocking the Free Press, controlling propaganda media and suppressing negative reports, are also forms of fascism.

Insecure, scared, struggling and/or racists people will often flock to a boisterous, charismatic icon to save them and eliminate perceived threats, often at the detriment of others.

'ANTIFA'- ANTI-FASCIST MOVEMENT

The antifa movement is composed of left-wing, autonomous, militant anti-fascist groups and individuals in the United States. The principal feature of antifa groups is their use of direct action, with conflicts occurring both online and in real life. Wikipedia

ANTIFA is seen as a 'Far-Left' group that is combative verbally and sometimes physically. They have a 'Fight Fire With Fire' ideology.

Who are Antifa? - ADL
https://www.adl.org › resources › backgrounders › who-are-antifa ▼
The anti-fascist protest movement known as **antifa** gained new prominence in the United States after the white supremacist Unite the Right rally in Charlottesville, VA, in August 2017.

Fascist Fricassee

Ingredients

2 Tbsp Butter or Olive Oil
16 oz Chicken Tenders
2 Carrots, sliced
8 oz Mushrooms, sliced
2 Cloves Garlic minced
2 Tbsp Flour
1 C Chicken Broth
1/2 C Heavy Cream
1/2 Tbsp Sage (ground)
1/2 Tbsp Fennel (ground)
2 Tbsp Fresh Parsley

Enjoy this old German favorite

Directions

Cook chicken well oiled pan until lightly browned. Remove from pan and set aside. Add carrots, garlic and peas to pan and cook until tender. Add mushrooms and cook for another 3 minutes. Add flour, stir. Add chicken broth, stir well. Add chicken breasts back to pan and cook for another 3-4 more minutes Add heavy cream and lemon juice. Cook for another 5 minutes. Remove from heat so sauce can thicken. Sprinkle with chopped parsley, salt and pepper to taste.

Trump Campaign Rally, "GET 'EM OUTTA HERE! And Don't Be Gentle"

Encouraging violence against peaceful protesters is just one form of fascism.

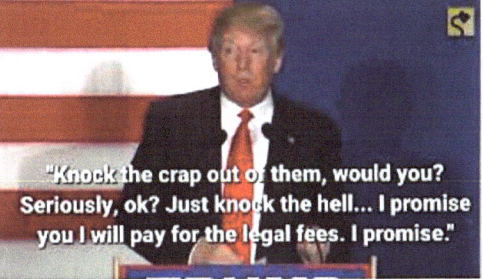

Republicans rally around their leader and are OK with immigrant families being separated, detained INDEFINITELY in cold cages with improper facilities, food, supplies and medical care. They believe Trump's constant rhetoric of "FAKE NEWS" and Main Stream Media being the "Enemy of the People." Police brutality towards minorities is also OK with them as Trump actually encourages it.

Democrats are horrified and appalled at what America has become and urge more people to vote in 2020.

FYI Snake Saute

JUST A FEW OF THE BILLS DEMOCRATS HAVE BROUGHT TO THE HOUSE FLOOR WITH NANCY PELOSI IN CHARGE	PASSED BY DEMOCRATIC HOUSE?	GIVEN A VOTE BY REPUBLICAN SENATE?
HR 1 -- Anti-corruption legislation to get big money out of politics	YUP	NOPE
HR 7 -- Ensures that women are paid equally to men for the same work	YUP	NOPE
HR 8 -- Requires anyone selling a gun to run a background check on the buyer	YUP	NOPE
HR 987 -- Reduces the cost of prescription drugs	YUP	NOPE
HR 1585 -- Reauthorizes the Violence Against Women Act	YUP	NOPE
HR 1644 -- Ensures ISPs provide equal access to the Internet	YUP	NOPE
HR 1994 -- Helps people save more for retirement	YUP	NOPE

When Republicans Whine That House Dems Are "Getting Nothing Done," Show Them This

Viral video shows border wall being scaled at Mexicali. Border Patrol says system 'worked exactly as designed'

Brian De Los Santos Palm Springs Desert Sun
Published 10:48 p.m. ET Dec. 5, 2019 | Updated 2:17 p.m. ET Dec. 6, 2019

FUN FACT

The "Do Nothing Dems" have passed numerous Bills through the House, such as; Voter Security, Equal Pay, Gun Control, Medication Cost Reductions, ect. Those Bills still sit with Mitch McConnell in the Republican controlled Senate.

FUN FACT

Trump Admin Reduces Funding, Restricts Access for People in Need.

SNAP — Supplemental Nutrition Assistance Program

GOP silent after State Department exonerates Hillary Clinton in email 'scandal' So is the media that ran endless email stories.

Mexico still isn't paying for the wall. But here's where the money is coming from.

Washington (CNN) The US Department of Defense is diverting an estimated $3.6 billion in military construction funds to help build President

"To say no to President Trump would be saying no to God"
Trump appoints Evanelicist to White House

and where I stand is holy.

FUN FACT

TIME

Why President Trump Cut a Methane Regulation That Even Big Oil Companies Wanted to Keep

The Trump Administration announced Thursday the rollback of an .... These companies acknowledge climate change is real and say they ...

Aug 29, 2019

FYI Snake Saute

Ingredients

3 Medium Swamp Snakes (can substitute w/Chicken Tenders)
1/4 C Olive Oil
1/4 tsp Paprika
1/4 tsp Chili Powder
1/4 tsp Garlic Powder
1/4 tsp Cayenne Pepper

Snake, the 'other white meat'
Nothing says saute like - sssssssnake!

Directions

Rinse the snake pieces and arrange in a crockpot. Add olive oil and spices. Stir gently once or twice during cooking. Cook on LOW for 2 hours 3 hours until cooked and tender and not biting anymore.

SOCIALISM

A BIG, BAD WORD to some (especially to the GOP and people at FOX News)
The fact of the matter is...
Democratic Socialism is simply people paying into the government (taxes) for public benefit such as public schools, healthcare, community programs, roads, libraries, FEMA, police & fire depts. —It's what we've been doing all along...and will continue to do, despite Republican rhetoric.

FUN FACT

Since 1968 we have had 28 years of Republican presidents and 20 years of Democratic presidents.

INDICTMENTS
Republicans — 209
Democrats — 4

 Hillary Clinton @HillaryClinton · 8h
Someone should inform the president that impeachable offenses committed on national television still count.

"WAS THERE A QUID-PRO-QUO?" "YES" — "EVERYONE WAS IN THE LOOP, IT WAS NO SECRET." "...AT THE EXPRESS DIRECTION OF THE PRESIDENT OF THE UNITED STATES"

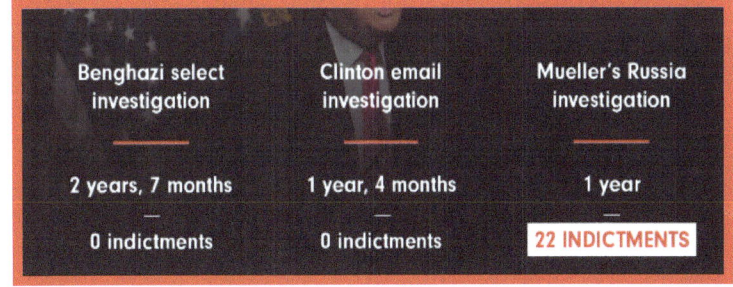

Benghazi select investigation	Clinton email investigation	Mueller's Russia investigation
2 years, 7 months	1 year, 4 months	1 year
0 indictments	0 indictments	22 INDICTMENTS

Republicans tend to have a very narrow range of newsfeeds (FOX News and Trump tweets).

Democrats tend to have numerous newsfeeds from a range of news outlets, but many important issues are buried under the pile of incoming political incidents. We all need to pay particular attention to CREDIBLE sources and engage in fact-checking regiments as foreign and domestic entities liter the airwaves with misinformation.

Shout-Out Sweet & Sour Peppers

Captain America
White House Invite—
No Thanks!

Megan Rapinoe and the U.S. women's team ...
washingtonpost.com

CBS News
Megan Rapinoe White House: U.S. women's national soccer team captain Megan Rapinoe refuses to go to…
Megan Rapinoe, co-captain of the U.S. women's soccer team, said she wouldn't visit the White House if the team wins the World Cup in a video ...
Jun 26, 2019

A Shout-Out To The 'Little People' With Big Voices

ABC News @ABC · 12m
Greta Thunberg at #UNGA: "This is all wrong... You all come to us young people for hope. How dare you!"
"You have stolen my dreams and my childhood with your empty words—and yet, I'm one of the lucky ones." abcn.ws/2IbXib3

"You shouldn't be looking to us kids to solve the climate problem!!!"

Bill of Rights: First Amendment
- Freedom of Religion
- Freedom of Speech
- Freedom of the Press
- Freedom of Expression
- Freedom to Peaceably Assemble
- Freedom to Petition

The New York Times
Greta Thunberg, Climate Activist, Arrives in N.Y. With a Message for Trump
The Swedish 16-year-old sailed across the Atlantic on an emissions-free yacht to speak at the U.N. Climate Action Summit next month.

58 WDJT
'Tired of seeing it:' Students speak out against gun violence at ...
MILWAUKEE (CBS 58) -- Students from 14 Milwaukee-area schools walked out of class on Friday, Dec. 13, protesting state gun laws.

WWL News, Talk, Sports Radio Station (blog)
Scoot: Did protests bring awareness to the national anthem?
NFL QB Colin Kaepernick took a knee on August 26, 2016 prior to a ... Anthem should be respected and there should be no protest during its ...

Shout-Out Sweet & Sour Peppers

Ingredients

1 lb Chicken Tenderloins
3 Tbsp Olive Oil
1 Red Onion
1 green pepper
1 red pepper

1 Orange Pepper
1 Pineapple (drained)
1/4 C Teriyaki Sauce
2 pinches Crushed Red Pepper

Don't let this sweet dish fool you. It packs quite a punch and delivers some serious goodness.

Directions

Rinse the chicken tenderloins and cut into smaller pieces. Dice the veggies, set aside. In a small bowl combined the teriyaki sauce, pineapple juice and cayenne pepper, set aside. Pour the olive oil into a wok or non-stick frying pan. Heat at medium-high. Cook the chicken first (thoroughly) then add in the veggies, cook until slightly tender. Pour the sauce over all and sprinkle the crushed red pepper. Heat another 5 minutes on low. Enjoy!

Congress shall make no law respecting an establishment of religion, or prohibiting the free exercise thereof; or abridging the freedom of speech, or of the press; or the right of the people peaceably to assemble, and to petition the Government for a redress of grievances.

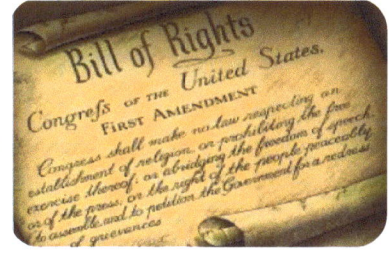

 Greenpeace @Greenpeace · 2h
Greta has done amazing work in calling for action on the #ClimateEmergency.
But don't forget Ridhima, Kaluki, Aditya, Nina, Autumn, Leah, or any of the other incredible young activists working for the future of this planet.
act.gp/30R3Xdl

Sierra Club @SierraClub · 8m
Greta Thunberg isn't the only trailblazing young climate leader. Activists from the Amazon to Nigeria share their ideas for battling the climate crisis: sc.org/2IMLsJ5

Republicans condemn peaceful protesters' voices that speak out against violence, climate change and other social issues.

Democrats continue to use peaceful protests to voice their opposition to infractions of civil liberties, inequality, health and environmental issues—all of which are protected by the Bill of Rights.

Assimilation Artichoke Dip

Cultural assimilation is the process in which a minority group or culture comes to resemble a dominant group or assume the values, behaviors, and beliefs of another group. **Wikipedia**

Reverse Assimilation

Native Americans forced to assimilate

Black Love: 10 Rappers Who Defied the ...

Fruit Loop Music

Cultural Assimilation, Cross Cultural Assimilation and Reverse Assimilation

It has been said that adjusting to a new culture, blending in, (assimilating) is best. Cultural clothing, language, habits and behaviors can be red flags, signaling that someone is...*different.* Some people are intrigued and curious while others, that operate on a more tribal level, are alarmed, defensive or hostile.

'Blending in' may help with acceptance, but some may feel they are betraying their true-selves and heritage. Then there are the ones who prefer to adopt a different cultural 'look' that they resonate with. The 'mixing and matching' of cultural styles, language, clothing, food, song and dance can be quite colorful and interesting.   clw

The Wide Spectrum of White Ra...
westcheddar.com

White Rappers Like th...

How many times have you heard this...

"My Grandmother on my father's side was Cherokee"

138   white rapper | Seb Is Hip Hop
sebishiphop.wordpress.com

Assimilation Artichoke Dip

Ingredients

2 Avocados
1 Tbsp Olive oil
1 Tbsp Lemon Juice
1/4 tsp Garlic powder
1/4 tsp Sea Salt

1 C Fresh Spinach
1 C Artichokes
(from jar, drained)

Toss it all together and see how it turns out. But don't worry, everything is OK. It'll be fun!.

Directions

Using a spoon, scoop the avocado flesh into a food processor. Add the olive oil, lemon juice, garlic, salt, pepper flakes, and several twists of black pepper. Blend until smooth, pausing to scrape down the sides as necessary. Add the spinach and artichokes and pulse until they are roughly chopped,

Republicans generally reject cultural differences and feel 'triggered' when seeing differences. One example: "The Dem's War on Christmas is over–You can say Merry Christmas again!"

Democrats generally respect cultural differences. Example: Happy Holidays is the preferred greeting, as it is 'ALL Inclusive' but no one thinks there's a "war on Christmas" and don't really care if it is said or not.

High Tech Biscuits

Now Entering Orbit: Tiny Lego-like Modular Satellites

Space is getting closer, thanks to small, cheap "satlets" that network themselves to solve problems in flight.

BY SARAH SCOLES 12.29.19 08:12 AM

smart railway opens in China ...
dailymail.co.uk

Futurism

Mysterious Swarms of Giant Drones Have Officials Baffled

Fleets of giant drones have been repeatedly spotted flying in the night sky over Colorado and Nebraska — and no one seems to know who they ...

1 day ago

AirForceTimes.com

The Space Force is officially the sixth military branch. Here's what that means.

About 16000 civilian and active duty personnel are now part of the Space Force, but the road to standing up the service is long.

1 week ago

It's A Win-Win With Clean, Green Cities

AFA: "Standing up a separate space bureaucracy amplifies the problem by driving more money to a headquarters function, not space operations."

Teslas, self-driving trucks, scooters: Transportation tech on display as San Antonio hosts mobility summit

The elementary-age Girl Scouts eagerly crowded around a table laden with shiny black helmets and tinted sunglasses in the parking lot outside ...

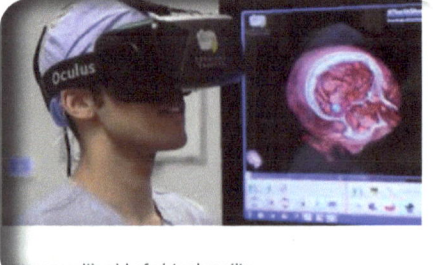

surgery with aid of virtual reality ...

Yahoo Finance

Fitbit (FIT) Partners WellCare to Reduce Type 2 Diabetes

Fitbit, Inc. FIT recently partnered with WellCare of Georgia, a WellCare Health Plans, Inc. company WCG, in order to help improve health culture ...

VR is not just for games! VR, tool for health, education and training

140

High Tech Biscuits

Ingredients

2 C Flour
1 tsp Baking Powder
3 Tbsp Butter, Olive Oil
1/2 Shredded Cheese
or Coconut Oil

1 Tbsp Chicken Bullion
1/2 tsp Garlic Powder
1/2 Rosemary
1/2 Fennel (Ground)
1/2 tsp Salt

Learn about technological advances and savor the taste of High Tech Biscuits

Directions

Mix dry ingredients, including shredded cheese, then add water and mix into a dough. Drop spoon fulls on to greased baking sheet. Bake at 395° for 10 minutes or until golden brown. Melt butter and drizzle lavishly over biscuits.

Countries of the Future Look Forward to 'Clean Cities,' Water Filtration, Green Energy Tech and Medical Advances.

S Asia Sentinel
Malaysia and the Lure of 'Smart Farming'
During an October trip to Azerbaijan, Prime Minister Mahathir Mohamad was wowed by a visit to a high-tech farm belonging Azersun, a major ...
4 weeks ago

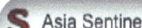

PRN PRNewswire (press release)
Human Horizons is Building a Smart City in Shanghai with ...
Human Horizons is Building a Smart City in Shanghai with High-tech Roads, Autonomous Driving Buses, and 5G Network ...

Singapore: New Jewel Changi Airport is ...

Singapore airport is a popular vacation attraction with botanic gardens, infinity pools, upscale eateries and theaters

launches to the Great Pacific Garbage...

IT Irish Times
High-tech Floating Farm employs robots to milk the cows
Perhaps we should be looking to Floating Farm in Schiedam, the Netherlands, for the future of high-tech, sustainable and environmentally ...
2 weeks ago

Republicans are not interested in Green Technology Development or the US becoming the 'Green Manufacturing Leader' but they do enjoy their tech toys.

Democrats want the US to be the Green Technology leader of the world but it's not gonna happen any time soon. They, too enjoy high tech and will most likely dwell in a VR state until further notice. "Alexa, find my VR."

Evolution Edemame

> "The danger to society is not merely that it should believe wrong things,...but that it should...lose the habit of testing things and inquiring into them."
> — William Kingdon Clifford

> "Non-violence is the greatest force at the disposal of humankind"
> — Mahatma Gandhi, 2/10/1869 - 30/01/1948

MATTEL'S NEW DOLL CAN BE A BOY, GIRL, NEITHER, OR BOTH
Plus: 30 bikers visit a lemonade...
Read the collection ▶

Dan Rather @DanRather

I believe the Trump Presidency will not only be remembered for its outrages but as a time when millions of Americans woke from a slumber of apathy and acquiescence to reclaim the ideals of the nation.

10:51 AM · 10/19/19 · Twitter fo...

9NEWS Denver @9NEWS · 53m
8-year-old has raised more than $50,000 in care packages for homeless veterans

8-year-old has raised more than $50,000 in care pa...
At age 4, Tyler Stallings, who comes from a family of servicemembers, decided he wanted to do somethi...
🔗 9news.com

Some 'Food For Thought'

US Becomes Global Leader of Green Energy Tech & Manufacturing

Planned Parenthood Resources For All & Male Birth Control Pills

Bylaws - Corporations & Shareholders Need to be Accountable. Investing Without Liability is Bad! Profit Over Health Must End. Corporations Give Back to Community and Pay Their Fair Share.

Fewer Desperate People = Fewer Desperate Acts
Living Wage, Higher Education and Universal Healthcare

Clean Air, Clean Water and Land
Healthcare for All
Jobs and Education
Peacetime and Travel
Exploration and Compassion
EVOLUTION

Greenpeace @Green... · 5h
Listen up, bankers.

The finance sector has done enough damage already.

You need to step away from coal, oil and gas, and stop fuelling the #climatecrisis, now.

Bank chief Carney issues climate change warning

MindShift @MindShiftKQED · 10m
Beliefs, values, and actions will spread the farthest and be tightly reinforced when everyone is communicating with everyone else.

What Makes a Good School Culture?
It starts with connections — strong and overlapping interactions among all members of the school community.

Funny how your quality of life improves dramatically when you surround yourself with good, intelligent, kind-hearted, positive and loving people.

 **FUN FACT**

"There's nothing weak about kindness and compassion. There's nothing weak about looking out for others. There's nothing weak about being honorable."
— Barack Obama

Rick Smith @ChiTownsOracle

As I'm in line waiting to get my flu shot, a Latino family is talking to the pharmacist about some scripts, no insurance, grandma has serious health problems and can't afford it. Grandma started crying, so did I....so I paid for her scripts and I got a standing ovation..

Evolution Edemame

Ingredients

1 Pkg Angle Hair Pasta
1/2 Pkg Edemme (1 Cup)
1 C Fresh, Raw Baby Spinach
3 Garlic Cloves (sliced)

1/2 C Pesto
3 Tbsp Olive Oil
Fresh Shredded Parmesan

Evolve and enjoy the 'Green Way' of life.

Directions

Boil the angle hair pasta until tender (15 min). Set aside. Simmer Olive Oil, Pesto, Edemame and Garlic in sauce pan on medium heat (7-8 min). Add in pasta, mix, then gently add spinach and top with fresh shredded Parmesan cheese.

> **Derek Johnson** @derekjGZ · Mar 20
>
> $7,610,350 every hour of every day for 30 years.
>
> That's what America will spend on its hoard of world-ending nuclear weapons. $2 trillion to fight a nuclear war no one can win.
>
> Imagine what we could do — who we could be — if we invested in creation instead of mass destruction.

Don't Let The Ugly In Others Kill The Beauty In You

FUN FACT

Old Coal Town Turns Green Brings Back Prosperity

Rural community that lost two coal mines is now teaching kids to instal... A program in Colorado's Delta County aims to ensure a brighter future for the next generation.

Republicans seem to prefer 'de-volution' and returning to some time in the past. Trump Supporters often refer to a time with less civil rights, women's rights, less regulation and government oversight. USA! USA! USA! Though after 3 years, it is still unclear as to what time period they refer.

Democrats embrace a Progressive ideology that includes equal rights for all, stricter environmental protection laws and Universal Healthcare.   Less Violence—More Compassion. Less Tribalism—More Social Evolution.

Voter Veggie Wrap

Sen. Debbie Stabenow ✓ @SenStabenow · 21h
Last week, @SenateDems brought seven bills to the floor that would secure our elections from foreign interference and protect your vote. Senate Republicans blocked all seven!

It is long past time @senatemajldr gets serious about the future of our democracy.

FUN FACT

Bergen County recounts votes in four ...

SENATE REPUBLICANS ARE STILL BLOCKING EFFORTS TO SECURE OUR ELECTIONS

PoliticsVideoChannel @politvidchannel · 54m
BREAKING: Senate Republicans blocked not one but two election security bills today that would have provided funding for states to shore up election security and created more transparency around online advertisements.

Why would the **GOP** Be against this?

FUN FACT
States are stepping up to help ensure voters get properly registered and their vote gets counted

GLITCHY VOTING MACHINES CHANGING VOTES

Bernie Sanders ✓ @B... · 5m
There is no "voter fraud" crisis. There is a voter suppression crisis because of cowardly Republicans who don't believe in democracy.

AJC ✓ @ajc · 1d
#BREAKING: About 330,000 voter registrations could be purged in Georgia. #gapol bit.ly/2BS8fHT

Voting machine switches v...

Voting Machines Changing Votes - YouTube

Voter Veggie Wrap

Ingredients

- Spinach Tortilla
- Whatever Meat or Veggie Slices
- Cheese (slice)
- Tomato
- Cucumber
- Red Onion
- Sage (ground)
- Whatever Dressing you like, just chose it!
- Salt & Pepper

Directions

Wrap it up and take it on the go if you have to, just make sure you vote!

Smear some dressing on the tortilla and wrap it all up. Let's get this done!

Risks of touch screen voting machines:
- can steal identity & change votes
- easily hackable & not auditable
- too expensive & very unreliable

Hand-Marked Paper Ballots! #1 Choice of cyber security experts

ONE MAN • ONE VOTE

The Electoral College is obsolete and should not be able to override the Will of the People (Majority Vote).
Get rid of it!

VOTE LIKE YOUR RIGHTS DEPEND ON IT

Former Secretary of State Hillary Clinton said she doesn't believe President Donald Trump will be reelected for a second term, calling him a "threat" to the United States and a "corrupt human tornado."

Joe Biden @JoeBiden · 10h
Let's be clear, President Trump is trying to hijack this election.
This isn't a Democratic issue or a Republican issue. This is a national issue.

president isn't telling the truth.

Voter Security Will Be A Hot Issue For The 2020 Election

- Republicans are OK with Senate Majority Leader, Mitch McConnell blocking Voter Security Bills. They are also OK when voting machines (past and present) "malfunction." (it is in Republican favor, for some reason)

- Democrats have suffered from extensive Gerrymandering, misinformation warfare, voter fraud and "malfunctioning" and hacked voting machines. The antiquated Electoral College has also stepped in when elections were close, to award Republican candidates despite a majority of Democratic votes.

Lest We Forget Trump Chocolate Cake

lest
/lest/

conjunction FORMAL

with the intention of preventing (something undesirable); to avoid the risk of.
"he spent whole days in his room, headphones on lest he disturb anyone"

- (after a clause indicating fear) because of the possibility of something undesirable happening; in case.
"she sat up late worrying lest he be held up on the way home"
synonyms: in case, just in case, for fear that, in order to avoid, to avoid the risk of

During the 'Age of Information' we find it harder to forget history, as well as the plethora of current events. With mini-super computers at our finger tips, we can 'Google' literally anything we'd like to know and learn. We do, however, need to *'consider the source,'* as the age of **misinformation** also takes firm hold.

MAGA - Make America Great Again. Some chant this at Trump rallies while others are still wondering what time period they are referring to. It was not the Obama's inheriting the 9/11 fall-out, Bush Wars and Recession, nor was it the recovery to a healthy economy with newly imposed regulations. It was not of Clinton's record economy with surplus and peacetime. Was it the time of 'Trickledown' Reaganomics? Was it the Nixon-Watergate times? Was it the Vietnam Wars?

At this time in US History we find ourselves at a tipping point where consequential decisions will be made and the repercussions, or benefits from the Trump Administration will be felt for decades. The Trumpland Cookbook is filled with information that is seen by some as "deplorable" while, inversely, others see as "Winning."

The divide is strong and grows thicker everyday. Regardless of your particular point of view, it is apparent some changes need to be made. Let us not forget, on which this nation was founded and adjust accordingly to modern times.

As this volume is being published, Trump awaits an Impeachment Trial and has just assassinated a prominent Iranian leader. Iran has put an 80 million dollar 'hit' out on Trump and vows retaliation.

clw

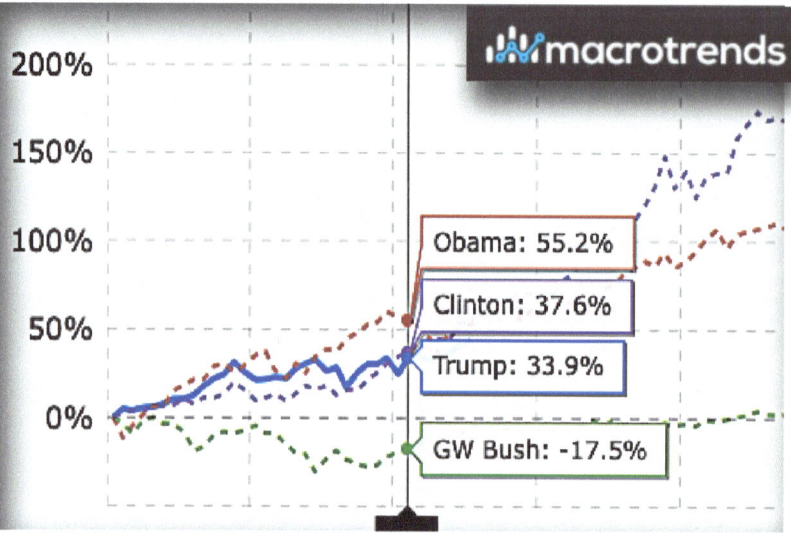

The Last Four Presidents' Economic Gains at 3 Years into Their Presidency

Clinton 37%, Bush -17%, Obama 55%, Trump 33%

Lest We Forget Trump Chocolate Cake

Ingredients

Chocolate Cake Mix
Chocolate Pudding Mix
Eggs

Water
Mini Chocolate Chips
Chocolate Frosting

Directions

"Its the best, most beautiful chocolate cake you've ever seen! It was this thick and it was the best"

Follow chocolate cake recipe on the box, but add pudding mix and sprinkle mini chocolate chips on top of frosting.

 Weird handshakes and misprounciations are one thing—blatant lies and corruption are another. Lets choose wisely.

D Deadline
President Donald Trump Calls For Investigation Into Obama Book Deals

Kenneth P. Vogel ✓
@kenvogel

N Newsweek
Fox News Was Attacking Barack Obama for Using Dijon Mustard at This Point in His Presidency

Trump remembers details of cake he was eating while launching missiles, but not which country he was attacking.

Donald Trump isn't the only president to have faced harsh criticisms just months into office. At this point in former President Barack Obama's ...
Jun 9, 2017

HRC was investigated several times regarding her emails and every time was fully cleared, while GOP members continue to violate security protocol by using private servers and personal cell phones for government business.

FUN FACT

Republicans are looking forward to prosperity, strict immigration laws and "a big beautiful wall!" that Mexico will pay for. They feel that their guns are safe under Trump (even though Trump was actually the only sitting President that said, "Maybe we take their guns early. Due Process later").

Democrats remember the high cost of the Bush Wars and the Recession of 2007.
They also remember the Civil Rights Movement and Fascists Nazi Regimes.   ~ *Lest We Forget*

147

The Boil Down

FOX News continues to spread false claims, though some Fox hosts have resigned.

Donald J. Trump ✓ @realDonaldTrump · 8h
Nervous Nancy Pelosi is doing everything possible to destroy the Republican Party. Our Polls show that it is going to be just the opposite. The Do Nothing Dems will lose many seats in 2020. They have a Death Wish, led by a corrupt politician, Adam Schiff!

THE DIVIDED STATES OF AMERICA - DIVIDED WE STAND
Citing Irreconcilable Differences

Would This Be Our Fate?

The beginning of 2020 has most people on edge worrying about the effects of climate change, the stock market, tariffs, healthcare, mass shootings, asylum seekers in cages, political scandals and volatile foreign relations (World War III).

Trump Supporters remain smitten about their "chosen one" and continue to chant during Trump campaign rallies. People across the nation wait with anxious anticipation to learn the results of the upcoming 2020 Presidential Election.

Newly Approved Voting Machines ...

PARTICIPATE

Current Hot Topics In The US

Heading into the 2020 Presidential Election

EPA/Climate Change (Prevention & Recovery)

TAXES - 1%ers & Corporations Paying Fair Share

Education (Public Access & Affordability)

Affordable Housing & Food

Affordable Healthcare For All

Foreign Relations & National Security

Shootings, Hate Crimes & Gun Control

Misinformation & Election Hacking

Internet Privacy & Data Breeches

Corporate Greed

It's Not About Left & Right - It's About Right & Wrong

Ask Yourself, Where Do You Stand?

...And Where Can You Compromise?

Thoughtful feedback, corrections and/or opinions are welcome.
Send inquires and comments to publishing@persuasivedesign.com

Volume 3 to be published December 2020 (hopefully)

www.ingramcontent.com/pod-product-compliance
Lightning Source LLC
Chambersburg PA
CBHW042246100526
44587CB00002B/39